MATCHED: A Memoir

Denise Massar

Copyright © 2024 by Denise Massar
Cover Design © 2024 Samantha Birks

Selected excerpts from *Matched* have been previously published in *HuffPost*, *Mutha Magazine*, and *Raise Magazine*.

All rights reserved. No part of this publication may be reproduced, distributed, or transmitted in any form or by any means, without prior written permission.

While this work is a memoir, many names have been changed to protect the privacy of individuals.

Golden State Publishing
August 2024

Matched: A Memoir / Denise Massar -- 1st ed.

For Jack, Kate, and Henry
Being your mom is the best part of my life.

LOSING

1

"The fetus is small for nine weeks," Dr. Chu said.

"Can she take vitamins?" Pete asked.

Jesus Christ. *Vitamins?* I wanted to scream in my husband's face, *Our baby is DEAD, you fucking idiot!*

"The baby should be bigger, and we should hear a heartbeat," Dr. Chu said. She'd been moving the wand over my belly but had stopped. "We'll do a blood test to confirm, and we'll know for sure tomorrow morning. I'll call you by nine with the results." She squeezed my arm and left the room.

Pete and I had driven to the appointment separately. I'd dressed knowing we'd meet up in the courtyard and he'd be checking me out from afar. I wore a black jersey skirt that swung around my thighs in a flirty way and a skinny tank that accentuated my newly fuller breasts. Pete liked the curves pregnancy added to my normally angular frame. I pressed into him when we hugged, feeling the Southern California sunshine on my shoulders and a surge of warmth between my legs.

"Who'd have thought we'd be *here* again?" we'd said.

Dr. Chu called just before nine the next day, saying my hormone levels were high, and for a moment, I let myself believe we'd escaped.

"Your levels are high because your body doesn't know the fetus has died; you're still creating pregnancy hormones and most likely will until you have the surgery to remove it.

"Schedule the D&C within the next week," she said, giving me the number to call.

How could I have been so stupid? So smug? You couldn't let the universe know when you were flying high. Everyone knew that. She'd swing her lighthouse head around, cast her beam on you, and you'd get the call that someone had lost a job, entered hospice, or a fetus had stopped growing. It was best to fly below the radar. *Play it cool.* I hadn't played it cool. We hadn't told family and friends yet, but I'd found every opportunity to tell strangers. Running a mud run at eight weeks, I'd avoided the obstacles, patting my belly as I ran by and yelling to the course staff, "Running for two!"

I thought back to the day before. How I'd purred up against my husband. The skirt, the tank top, the Rocket Dogs. I was replicating the way I'd dressed when I was pregnant with our firstborn, Jack, imagining that if I could dress the same, look the same, then we could still *be* the same people we were four years ago: young, carefree—even pregnant! It would be like we'd never left California. (We'd done a two-year stint in the Midwest to advance our careers in textbook publishing. Iowa had been particularly hard on us—the long, cold winters had given our new marriage a nasty case of frostbite we were still trying to thaw out.) But I was a fraud. We weren't young; I was forty, Pete forty-six. We weren't carefree; we had two kids under five. And now we weren't pregnant.

I'd been careless. Was it the blue cheese dressing on Jack's salad? I'd been so nauseated, it was the first thing that had looked good in two days, and I just inhaled it. Was it when the pedicurist at Happy Nails started to massage my ankle? She'd barely touched it when I yelled out, "No!" But there was a pressure point that, if massaged, could cause a spontaneous miscarriage, right? I'd heard that. Or had it been the mud run? The field had been so deep and viscous that I'd lost a shoe in the muck. I knew you could work out while pregnant, but why did I always feel the need to *prove that* to everyone?

My mom, Jenny, came from Boise to help with Jack and Kate, four and two, before the D&C. I handed her the reins and hid in our bedroom upstairs. Channel surfing, I landed on *Contact* with Jodi Foster and Matthew McConaughey.

Has there ever been an on-screen couple with less chemistry? And what's with Jodi's Mary Todd Lincoln ringlets in the party scene? Stupid. I could do better.

I sent my friend Marcia a text: "Time to talk?"

Marcia's first two pregnancies had ended in miscarriage, and she'd learned the way I had, at the nine-week appointment. When I found out I was pregnant, I stopped calling or texting her and crossed my fingers that she wouldn't notice. I didn't want any of her miscarriage juju rubbing off on me.

Marcia (pronounced Mar-see-uh) and I met at Central Washington University. I first saw her in the dining hall where everyone studied at night. She was standing next to a table full of guys from Bainbridge Island. The Bainbridge guys wore fleeces and drove muddy Toyota 4Runners. They went camping in the Cascades or floated the Yakima with a twenty-four pack and a bong, on a moment's notice. They intimidated me. I wasn't a camping-on-a-moment's-notice kind of girl. Marcia was. And she was beautiful. Half Japanese, half white, she had creamy skin and full lips the color of Rainier cherries. Her black hair fell in waves to the middle of her back. Her laughter was generous and unladylike. The Bainbridge boys were laughing at whatever she was saying and calling her *Marsh*, wanting to be familiar with her like that. She was one of the guys, but they all wanted to fuck her, too. I hated her on sight. And vowed to make her my best friend.

She called from her office in San Francisco.

"I was pregnant," I said. "But now I'm not."

"Oh, babe," she said.

We cried. Or she let me cry. And then, she told me what I could expect during and after the D&C. When she'd had hers—both of them—I hadn't dug too deep. I knew that afterward, her husband, CK, had driven her home. He hadn't really known what to say and ended up going to a late breakfast with his dad. And she'd been sad. I felt bad about not having asked more.

The D&C was on a Friday in April.

When I woke up, I could hear the movements of nurses behind the curtains on either side of me. I could smell latex and the clean, warm laundry smell of my blanket. Our fingers laced, Pete traced quick, compulsive circles on the top of my hand with his thumb. It was irritating. I wanted him to comfort me the way Mom would, with a slow and steady caress. But through his jittery touch, I felt his fear of being unable to protect me and his sense of helplessness in losing the child we'd begun to dream about but would never meet.

"I'm fine," I said, squeezing his hand.

On the way home, we stopped at our favorite Thai place in our old neighborhood, wanting to be somewhere enclosed, dim, familiar. We took a booth, and the waitress placed steaming cups of jasmine tea in front of us.

"How are you?" I asked.

"I'll be okay," he said. "I'm worried about you."

Growing up, "dramatic emotion" wasn't encouraged. One of Mom's admonishments that caused me deep embarrassment was, *"Stop being so dramatic."* Pete was cut from similar cloth. The youngest of five, he learned to make his case intelligently and forcefully, but there was little time for drama. I'm a Major People Pleaser. I like to show people how low-maintenance I can be. When I was in the hospital delivering Kate, the nurse asked me to tell her where I was, pain-wise, using the chart on the wall. Zero was "Not hurting," and showed a happy, smiling face. Ten was, "Hurts the worst you can imagine," and showed a crying face contorted with pain. My daughter's head was crowning, and the doctor had just slipped his scalpel into my vaginal opening and dragged the blade two inches toward my anus to give my daughter the room she needed to make her exit. There'd been no time for an epidural.

"Where 'ya at with the pain, hon?" the nurse had asked. And I chose eight, "Hurts a whole lot," because choosing ten just seemed dramatic.

"I'm fine," I said to Pete, ripping the tops off three sugars.

But I didn't want to be easy or accommodating. I didn't want any pieces left unsaid, waiting to be spoken until *the next right moment*. I took a sip of my tea.

"Having a third baby was…you said you were done, but you were *so excited*. We saw Jack and Kate as big brother and big sister to this baby, and we fell in love with that—that picture of them. *This baby was never supposed to happen*. And I've been holding up little hoodies, and now what?" I asked, raising empty hands, wanting my husband to give me a different answer than the one I already had. "He's just…*gone*?"

I dropped my hands and watched as tears fell and spread like ugly gray dye on the white paper napkin.

"I still want him," I said. "I just still really want him."

2

My older brother, Bob, was adopted in 1966, and I was adopted in 1972. In between, my parents adopted a baby girl they named Debbie. Debbie died just before her second birthday. The understanding among extended family and friends was that she died of SIDS. SIDS is listed as the cause of death on her death certificate.

When Debbie was a baby, my Dad, Dewey, was the head park ranger at Fort Canby State Park. Fort Canby ran along the coastline of the southwestern tip of Washington State, where the Columbia River fed, churning and spitting, into the Pacific. Dad, Mom, Bob, and Debbie lived in what had once been the North Head lighthouse keeper's house. Two stories tall and built to withstand volatile weather, the white house with brick walls a foot-and-a-half thick sat on a rocky jut 150 feet above the ocean. Some lighthouses signal dangerous coastlines, hazardous reefs, or hidden rocks, while others mark a safe harbor. The lighthouse at North Head signaled danger.

"Didn't it terrify you—living on a cliff?" I asked Mom after I had kids and realized that, *Holy shit*, my mom had lived on a cliff 150 feet above the ocean with two toddlers.

"Not really. There was a big fence—six, seven feet tall and military-grade. The thing was the gate; we were forever reminding people to close it when they left. I was more worried about the windows with you kids (*'You kids' could be any combination of Bob, Debbie, and me throughout her life. Though I'm not yet born in this story, I'm still in the mix.*). The bedrooms were upstairs, and the windowsills were just a few inches off the floor. If one of you would've fallen…So, I put two-by-fours over the bottom half of your windows and painted them white."

North Head was almost always enshrouded in a cold, damp beach fog that settled on your skin. It didn't burn off, exposing the sun's warming rays; it rose like a curtain, revealing a grey and indifferent sky.

"They said there were a lot of suicides up there. Especially women," Mom said. "I used to drive down to Naselle and sit on a picnic bench just to feel the sun on my face."

The first lighthouse keeper, Alexander Pesonen, moved into the house in 1888 and, shortly after, married a twenty-year-old Irish woman named Mary Watson. Mary and Alexander lived at North Head for more than twenty-five years. They were isolated. The rain came in sideways. Howling winds were recorded at 160 miles per hour. Due to unpredictable conditions, shifting sandbars, and rocky reefs, ships aiming for the mouth of the Columbia capsized so often that the stretch of ocean outside Mary's kitchen window was dubbed 'The Graveyard of the Pacific.' The bodies washed up in the cove below her house. The sun refused to comfort. In the spring of 1923, Alexander took Mary to Portland, one-hundred miles inland, to see a doctor. Diagnosed with "melancholia," she stayed in Portland to receive treatment but returned to North Head in the first part of June. Her first morning home, Mary woke at five a.m., put on her coat, walked out the door, and flung herself off the cliff.

Debbie was sick a lot. Her lungs were always congested, so Mom and Dad stacked books under the head of her crib to prop her up and help her breathe. They thought it might be cystic fibrosis for a while, but that was eventually crossed off the list.

But in December of 1970, she got pneumonia. When she began seizing, Mom and Dad rushed her to the shoebox of a hospital in Ilwaco. The doctor they knew there, Dr. Nease, said *not to worry, probably roseola, she'll be fine*. But the other doctor, Mom noticed, offered no reassurances. They worked on her throughout the night in a room so small—a converted broom closet—that Mom and Dad couldn't be in Debbie's room when the doctors and nurses were with her. When they couldn't be at her bedside, Mom and Dad sat in a waiting area directly across from her room.

During the night, as her condition worsened, Dr. Nease told them, "If we can get her through sunrise, the odds are in our favor."

Mom knew before she knew. The tingling started in her scalp—a searing electrical current shot down through her arms, legs, and feet, accompanied by a crushing sense of fear. She'd been slumped in the plastic waiting room chair but sat up. "*Go see...*" she said to Dad.

Debbie died at sunrise.

Mom's parents drove down from Olympia, her aunts from Pe Ell. Dad's parents came up from Longview. His mom ironed Debbie's dress.

"Did you pick her clothes?" I asked Mom. "Or did you want someone else to do it?"

"Oh no, I wanted to do it. She was mine to take care of. I took out her blue dress and her patent leather shoes. The pendant Doc and Rita had given her with her initials on it. I've always felt bad about the patent leather. I wish I'd put her in little slippers."

Mom doesn't remember any of the funeral. She doesn't remember much about the months after other than she'd drop my brother at preschool and wander around town. She remembers asking *"Why?"* of shopkeepers and coffee-shop girls. She remembers watching trials in the courthouse to have somewhere to be.

I didn't really understand who Debbie was to Mom and Dad, or what they'd lost, until my firstborn, Jack, turned two. They hadn't lost a silent infant swaddled in a blanket, as I'd always imagined her; they'd lost their little girl who giggled. Their girl who'd been so proud because her hair had just grown long enough for 'big-girl' ponytails.

The doctors shaved one of her ponytails off that night as they frantically searched for a vein.

If you're wondering if I grew up feeling like a replacement baby, I didn't. Mom had a way of making me feel like I was her favorite person in the world. I always felt loved. *Special*. I knew she carried grief for Debbie alongside her love for me, but I didn't feel like those two things were mixed up in each other.

I didn't feel like a substitute for Debbie, but I did feel like there was a ghost of sorts in our family. There wasn't much in our home to give me clues about this little girl my entire family had loved, but I'd never met. "Debbie's your sister," Mom told me. But it didn't feel true. I wanted her to be, but how could she be my sister if I'd never met her? My parents kept the black tin box on the top shelf of their closet. It's where Mom kept everything Debbie: her birth certificate, photos, cards people had sent, her death certificate. I'd sneak the box down and hide on the far side of my parents' bed to look at pictures of her. My favorite was an 8 x 10. It was black and white, which made her seem like a baby from long ago, though she would've been just four years older than me. In it, she sits up with her legs splayed, the skirt of her cotton dress resting lightly on her bare knees. I'd study her face and body for signs of sickness. She had dark, kind of spiky hair; I thought maybe that was a sign. She looked happily, sweetly not into the camera but just right of it. I knew she was looking at Mom.

The first of December, Mom would bring the Christmas card tree down from the attic. It was an old tree branch she'd spray-painted white and stuck in an MJB coffee can. The base of the branch was supported by rocks my brother had collected from the tree farm across the street, and the coffee can was covered in aluminum foil and garnished with a big red bow. The idea was that you'd tape cards to the branches as you received them, and by Christmas, you'd have a big, full tree. The tree sat in the same spot every year, on top of the Magnavox—our stereo the size of a canoe—that lined a wall in the dining room. Bob and I would take turns getting the mail and taping on the cards. When it was my turn, I'd run out to the mailbox at the end of our gravel driveway the second the mailman drove away. Then I'd open the cards, spreading them out on our Oscar the Grouch-green shag carpet and organize them, favorite to least. I favored cuddly woodland animals. Mom had a soft spot for Currier & Ives. If a card had glitter, it immediately went into the first-place position. Ranking complete, I'd get the Scotch Tape out of the china closet and tape the day's card onto the branches. When Bob and I were younger, we'd fight over whose turn it was; but as he got older, he didn't really care. The lack of competition diluted my joy a little, but mostly, I was happy to put every card exactly where I saw fit.

Every year, Seattle Children's Hospital sent us a Christmas card, acknowledging that Mom's dad had made a donation to their SIDS research center. The card thrilled and scared me. It pleased me that I was in the loop enough to know it was about Debbie and that I should approach the card with reverence. It scared me because the logo for Seattle Children's Hospital (or maybe just Seattle Children's SIDS research?) bore an infant with its arms sticking straight out from its shoulders, its torso and legs swaddled in a white muslin-like cloth. The baby's head, the outstretched arms, and the swaddled torso and legs made a perfect cross. I didn't know—was the baby supposed to be dead? It looked like the kind of cloth that might be used for burial. But why would they send such a sad card to thank people for sending them money? Was it supposed to make you have feelings of Jesus? It was hard to tell, and I wasn't gonna ask.

Every year, the card came with the dead baby, which in my mind was Debbie, and I taped it to our tree.

SIDS was a catch-all for baby deaths of unknown causes in the 1970s. By today's medical standards, any baby over the age of one wouldn't be ruled a SIDS death. When I was older, Mom told me that Debbie's pediatrician said that Debbie died because she had a grossly underdeveloped vascular system—the system of a seven-month-old fetus—and it just couldn't keep up with her nearly two-year-old body any longer. He told her the most likely reason for an underdeveloped vascular system was maternal drug use during pregnancy, and in Debbie's case, he thought her birth mom had probably used cocaine.

Seven-foot-high chain-link fence, brick walls a foot-and-a-half thick, boards over windows.

Close the gate close the gate close the gate.

Nothing Mom and Dad did could have saved her. Debbie was always going to die.

3

In the late sixties and early seventies, when Bob and I were adopted, all domestic adoptions were closed, which meant the adoptive families were given only a vague idea of what the birth parents were like, and the birth parents weren't given any information about who would raise their baby. Of Bob's biological family, Mom remembers being told that the biological father was in the Navy and that, "You and Dewey couldn't do so good yourselves!" About my biological mom, they were told, "Sixteen, nice family." About Debbie's birth parents they were given no information at all.

But in the early spring of 2013, Dad received a letter from Debbie's biological mom. The gist of the letter was that she'd always wondered about the baby she'd given up forty-five years before—was there anything they could share with her? Pictures? My parents had been divorced for thirty years by then; Dad was remarried, and my parents did not speak. So, when Dad got the letter, he called Bob and me. *What did we think?* Did we want him to share the letter with Mom? Our shared reaction was an immediate, *"No way."* Mom had never fully healed from Debbie's death. She does not—is not able to—keep pictures of Debbie on display. *Why bring up anything that would upset her?* And I knew, in a way that Bob and Dad didn't, that Debbie's biological mom would be an unwelcome person in Mom's life even if Debbie had lived. Debbie was *hers*. But she didn't live. And she didn't live because her birth mom had used hardcore drugs while she was pregnant, and maybe had or hadn't disclosed that information when she placed her baby for adoption. So, no, Mom didn't want to meet Debbie's birth mom or share any part of Debbie with her.

I asked Dad if he had the same memory of the pediatrician telling them that Debbie's death was the result of her birth mom's drug use. He said he didn't remember clearly—maybe something like that, he thought? But he did remember the undertaker telling him that Debbie's veins were the smallest he'd ever seen and that it had been very difficult to embalm her.

My thoughts upon hearing these things from Dad were: *How can two people have such different memories of being told the cause of death for their daughter? How can Dad's understanding of what killed his daughter be...foggy? And for chrissake, why would an undertaker say that to a grieving father?*

I told Pete about the letter. Here's what's great and also so incredibly hard about marriage: You marry someone who's had a whole different upbringing than you have; the way they interact with their family, their communication style, their understanding of *your* family— all completely different from your own. Pete approaches things from angles I would never consider. And sometimes I think he's really smart. Other times I think, *That is the stupidest fucking thing I've ever heard.*

Regarding the letter, Pete said, "You guys don't have the right to keep the letter from your mom—Debbie is her daughter. She deserves to see the letter and decide what she wants to do with it. Imagine if it was Kate? Give her the letter."

We gave her the letter.

Mom came to visit us in California shortly after. We were at the lake near our house, sitting on a picnic bench facing the water so we could watch the kids play on the shoreline.

"What'd you think of the letter?" I asked.

"I want nothing to do with *that woman*," she said.

I nodded as we watched Kate drag a plastic yellow shovel across the wet sand.

"And another thing," she added, with a cock of her head. "I need to thank Pete—I'm a helluva lot stronger than you guys gave me credit for."

Dad and his wife Donna ended up meeting Debbie's birth mom for coffee. I asked Dad how it went—did he ask about the drug use?

"Yeah, she said she lived a pretty rough life there for a while," he said.

Before meeting with Debbie's biological mother, Dad had asked me repeatedly if Mom had pictures of Debbie that he could bring along.

"She must have *something*," Dad said.

I thought about the tin box. The photos that were there with the other relics of my sister's short life.

"No," I answered. "She doesn't have anything."

After Mom returned home, the effects of the letter from Debbie's birth mom lingered. I was curious about the woman who'd written the letter. Birth moms were mysterious, almost fictional characters to me. I was sad for my parents, that painful memories had been dredged up. I'd even felt a pang of nostalgia when Bob, Dad and I had been on the phone talking about Mom. It had been nearly thirty years since it had been the four of us in any sense. After reading the letter a second time, I tossed it on my desk and went to the kitchen to get a cup of coffee. As I added spoonfuls of Coffee-Mate and sugar, the aroma changing from bitter to sweet, I thought about the letter, a grenade lobbed from 1970 into 2013. I thought about my own longings—to brush my lips across a downy head laying on my chest, to feel the perfect weight of a baby lifted from a bassinet.

It's been a year.

And then: Adoption. *Adoption.*

Long after our post-D&C dinner at Phuket Thai, Pete told me he'd been worried I might die during the procedure. He said the whole thing had been scary and sad and emotionally draining, and he didn't ever want to go through it again. The unattractive side of me found that a little funny—that the months of nausea, having the dead fetus vacuumed out, and the subsequent passing of blood clots the size and consistency of a sea cucumber had been draining on *him*. But I understood. Pete had been more worried about the D&C than I was because he didn't have a Marcia—someone who'd been there and could reassure him that while it would be horrible, I would be okay. After Pete shared his fears with me, I didn't bring up 'trying for another' again.

But, adoption. Why had it taken a stranger's letter for me to think about adopting our third child? We'd talked about adoption when we were dating, and one thing I'd loved about Pete was that he was totally into it. He had none of that "My Loins/My Sperm/My Genes" machismo thing going on that some men did. We agreed we'd adopt if we had any trouble conceiving, but we didn't, so the conversation hadn't come up again.

Pete had three solid, logical reasons why he didn't want to try for another pregnancy. One, he didn't want to go through another miscarriage and possible subsequent D&C. Two, he didn't want our baby to have Down syndrome or other chromosomal issues due to my age. And three, he felt we were simply too old to be starting over again. "You'll be 59, and I'll be 65 when he graduates high school," he said.

Adoption took away objections one and two, immediately. I worked in sales. If I could remove two out of three customer objections? I was movin' in for the kill.

One night, not long after, I put the kids to bed, and Pete and I met on the couch in our den. I had a bulleted Word document; I used to do that for our Big Talks in case I got flustered. I told him I was still aching from the miscarriage, not for *that* baby necessarily, but for a baby. I told him that feeling, that sense that we were meant to be a family of five had roosted and didn't seem to be going away. I told him we had more love to give. He took it all in, not saying a word until my presentation was complete.

"Give me some time to think about it," he said.

"Okay. (*Cautious elation, cautious elation, cautious elation*) How much time?" I asked.

"A couple months," he answered.

"So, like…around your birthday?" I asked.

"Yeah," he said. "That sounds right."

Fast forward two months and I'm standing in Dairy Queen cashing in Jack and Kate's meal coupons when my phone rings. It's Pete calling from the road.

"Hey," I said, pressing the phone to my ear with my shoulder, Dilly Bars in my hands.

"I've been thinking about what you said," he said, his voice steady and sure. "Let's do it."

SEARCHING

4

I Googled 'best adoption attorney in LA,' and Alan's name popped up. He'd been featured on KCAL 9, talking about adoption scams. I watched the video, studying Alan's voice and mannerisms. I couldn't find anything negative about him on the internet, just grateful reviews by happy new parents. I called his office the next day and made an appointment for May 21.

When we walked into Alan's office, I was disappointed. I figured someone who came up as the "best adoption attorney in LA" would have a nicer reception area. It was small. Just large enough for a couch and a chair around an oak coffee table. Old magazines. Dated furniture. The walls were decorated with pictures of hula dancers and tropical flowers. Pete picked up a flyer from the table that read, "Do You Have an Adoption Plan?"

Trying to ease our nerves he murmured, "If I know my wife, you already have an adoption plan."

"I don't even know what an adoption plan *is*," I whispered back.

A short, brunette woman came to escort us back.

Alan stood up from behind his desk to greet us. Tall, broad-shouldered, and rounded in the middle, his body type was jovial and authoritative all at once. He was balding on top with a slight comb-over and wore wire-rimmed glasses. He had a great smile—not a polite smile but a full-on grin. His desk was cluttered with stacks of folders, like my own at home. I liked him immediately.

He waved us into the two comfortable-looking tufted chairs in front of his desk. Part of what'd drawn me to Alan was that he was an adoptive father, and photos of his daughter were prominently displayed. He spoke about his wife, Vonnie, with great affection—not the way people do when they're trying to convince you they're happily married, but in the way you could tell that he genuinely got a kick out of her. Vonnie, it turned out, was the woman who'd just brought us back.

Taking his cue from the waiting room décor, Pete began talking about Hawaii; we were leaving for Oahu in a couple of weeks. Alan was full of insider tips and places to see. They bantered on for fifteen minutes while I sat, pen poised. *He's choosing this moment to be Mr. Chatty Social Guy?* He never did that—that was my role in the marriage. Alan's initial consultation fee was $385 per hour. We'd spent nearly a hundred bucks to chitchat about the best sushi in Honolulu. I tight-lipped smiled at Pete.

"I have a list of about fifteen questions, and Pete has a couple of questions as well," I said.

"How about I tell you everything I want to tell you about adoption today," Alan said, leaning back, folding his hands over his belly. "And then, at the end, if your questions are unanswered, we'll return to your yellow legal pad?"

With that, our adoption education began.

Every state had its own adoption laws, but in California, the actual transfer of parental rights would happen like this: In the hospital, the birth mom would meet with an intermediary who would go over the placement documents with her. Hopefully, before the baby was born, but sometimes after, the birth father would sign a document terminating his rights. Once we were home with our baby, the birth mom had thirty days to change her mind. A lot of birth moms waived that right—they didn't want or need the thirty days to be sure. (I desperately hoped our birth mom wouldn't want the thirty days.)

I liked the way Alan kept saying, "Your baby." It seemed audacious, like it was just a matter of time. His confidence gave me confidence. We'd spoken our hope for a baby out loud, and so far, no one thought it was crazy.

The discussion turned to birth moms. Alan's saying the words made my palms go clammy. Jennifer Gilmore's semi-autobiographical novel about her adoption search, *The Mothers*, was my bible, and she'd written about potential birth moms she'd spoken to, including scammers and skinheads. I had so many questions about this woman (girl?) that I needed but also feared. Would she need a lot of money? Would she stay with us? Be on drugs? Would her family members try to change her mind or want to come over for Thanksgiving? But my number one fear, by a zillion miles, was this: *Will she change her mind?* In a show I was obsessed with, *I'm Having Their Baby*—an adoption reality show on Oxygen—birth moms changed their minds about half the time.

Alan told us that, usually, a birth mom chose adoptive parents around the beginning of her third trimester. That would give us three months to get acquainted, typically meeting in a neutral place like a restaurant or park. The timeframe could be much shorter, he said—in very rare circumstances, a woman gave birth without an adoption plan ('adoption plan,' we learned, was just adoption-speak for when a birth mom has chosen parents for her baby.) In those cases, she selected parents for her baby from her hospital bed. We'd meet for the first time when we went to the hospital to pick up our son or daughter. I wanted *that* call. I wanted to leap right over stilted conversations around a splintering picnic table about what music Pete and I listened to in college.

Alan explained there were two approaches to finding a birthmother: We could rely on him solely to promote us and get us in front of birth moms (that was exactly what I planned to do), or we could tell friends and family we were hoping to adopt and ask them to help us find a baby. Promoting ourselves felt so *gauche*. I preferred to think of us waiting in a dignified manner until Alan called to tell us he'd found a baby. (I imagined receiving this call wearing a suit like Jackie O's pink Chanel, but mine was butter-yellow with white trim, my legs crossed demurely at the ankles.)

Then, Alan threw out a couple of statistics that quickly changed my mind: For every newborn available for adoption, there were eighty hopeful adoptive couples/singles vying for that baby. While Alan found about half of "birth mom situations," as he called them, the other half his clients found their birth mom on their own.

That scene from *When Harry Met Sally* popped into my head, when Carrie Fisher says to Meg Ryan, "The right man for you might be out there right now, and if you don't grab him, someone else will, and you'll have to spend the rest of your life knowing that someone else is married to your husband."

No one else was gettin' my baby.

My competitive nature sparked to life. My marketing side ignited. Alan was telling us that finding a birth mom was about writing a great Dear Birth Mom Letter—known as the DBML—and fearlessly marketing ourselves. If people were writing and marketing themselves toward their babies? If that was how the game was played?

Oh, I was gonna win this shit.

Alan broached the other question that loomed large in my head: *How long will it take?* I knew, logically, he couldn't give us an answer. But, secretly, I thought he might say: "You are an exceptionally attractive, well-rounded, and desirable family.

I expect you will be picked by one of the very first birth moms I present you to." And with a wink and a smile he'd add in a hushed tone, "I'd expect a baby in your family by the end of summer."

He did not say that.

He said we should expect to wait one to two years.

"Do you think our already having kids is going to be a deterrent to a birth mom?" I asked.

"To some, it will be, and to some, it won't," he said. "There are all kinds of birth moms—the ones who want their baby to be the only child and ones who want their child to grow up in a family with guaranteed siblings and would be attracted to a fuller, busier home."

I knew I'd fall into the latter category as a birth mom. Alan's explanation was comforting. Of course there were as many birth mom personalities as there were adoptive parent personalities. He thought we'd be a perfect match for some birth moms. He told me not to worry.

Alan closed the 'How long?' conversation with one of his favorite match stories. He was representing a gay couple, two men, and they'd just turned in the first draft of their Dear Birth Mom Letter. Alan made edits and suggestions for a second draft but kept a copy of their first. He began working with a new birth mom, a Black woman, at about the same time. Though it was still a rough draft, Alan presented the couple's Dear Birth Mom Letter to her. She loved them, picked them immediately. They became good friends and still saw each other often.

"You just never know," he said. "Buy a car seat, and have it ready."

Alan folded his hands on his desk and asked if we had any remaining questions.

"Is it going to affect our chances that I don't know my birth mom?" I asked. "I mean, we're talking about openness and how important it is to us that our baby knows his or her birth mom, but I don't know mine. That makes us sound insincere."

"No, I don't think so," Alan said. "If it comes up, you can talk about how you were adopted in a different time. Adoptions were very different then."

Relieved, I asked Alan the only question left on my list: "What should the tone of the letter be? Do we want to sound cool, hip, like we could be friends with her? Or should the tone be more parental?"

"You want to sound like the parents that she wants to be to her child but can't be," Alan said. "She wants to hear that you can give her child the things that she wants for them—a solid family life, a college education, vacations."

Pete had only one question, and I admired him for having the balls to ask it, because even though I wondered too, I couldn't have.

"What happens if the baby is deformed or has a condition like Down syndrome?" Pete asked.

"You have no responsibility to adopt the child," Alan said. "You are free to walk away. That has only happened once in my career, when the baby was severely deformed. The couple decided they could not adopt the child, and the mother ended up keeping the baby."

I felt guilty about feeling relieved. Possibly sensing my guilt, or maybe just delivering a line he'd delivered to hundreds of adoptive parents before us, Alan said, "You're not here to save the world; you're here to bring a healthy baby into your family."

I walked out of Alan's office in a totally different place than I'd been walking in. If we were responsible for finding our baby, I wanted to get on it *now*.

It was time to get to work.

5

How do you write a letter to someone to convince them to *give you their baby*? This letter of just a few pages needed to convey who Pete and I were as a couple, who we were as a family, what our extended family was like, and our general philosophy on life.

The pictures were the most important part of the letter. Alan said he'd seen birth moms glance at a photo and toss a DBML into the 'no' pile without reading a word. It sounded ruthless, but I got it. He also told us, specifically, to not go out and have family photos taken, "Candids are better," he'd said. So, I booked a two-hour session with a professional photographer the next day. I knew what he was saying, but we lived in Orange County; it was nearly a requirement that professional photos were taken to *look* like candids—easy, breezy, just another day at the beach.

Alan's guidelines on photos:

- No alcohol
- No wedding pictures
- No sunglasses
- No interior shots of your home (in case your style doesn't match theirs)
- No pictures with relatives (in case Uncle Greg comes across as pervy to a birth mom)

- No pictures where the kids take up your lap (Leave room for the birth mom to imagine *her* baby on your lap.)
- Show your fun side: costume parties, pictures of the two of you being silly/goofy!
- Husbands: smile with your teeth.

Before the session, I pored over the photos we already had. I chose one of Pete and me on our honeymoon in Cancun, arms draped easily around each other, our skin bronzed and young. Looking at the photo, I realized I hadn't seen Pete that relaxed in a long time. In another, a photo taken on our first date, we're crossing a finish line, covered head-to-toe in mud and holding hands. I'd invited Pete to do the San Dimas Muddy Buddy with me "as a friend." After the race—the mud dried to a light grey and caked to our bodies—we went to a Mexican restaurant, drank tart, on-the-rocks margaritas with salt, and told each other our stories. Pete gave me his University of Illinois ballcap for my mud-stiffened hair.

The photographer, Tracey, arrived at our house in the late afternoon. She was older, frizzy-haired, sweaty and scattered, but she was good with the kids and cool with the dog, so I was happy. The plan was to do the first shots in the front yard, then move on to the lake to get the beachy shots. We were shooting at two locations because I wanted "the whole family shot" to include our white lab, Cooper. Cooper was a major part of the Family Brand I was creating: fun, easy-going, Southern California beach family. Educated professionals who can offer stability but don't take ourselves too seriously! #doglovers #fit #casual

The shoot on our front lawn was a clusterfuck. Kate was being Kate, which meant running up into the camera and trying to get a little side BFF thing going with Tracey. Jack's truest, sweetest smile was a half-smile in which his lips barely curved upwards. *"Smile with your teeth!"* I told him, which hurt his feelings, so then, he couldn't really smile at all. Cooper wouldn't sit still, so Pete's face was set in a pinched wince in nearly every shot.

We headed to the lake. The first set-up Tracey wanted to do was of our family sitting on a rock wall with the moored sailboats serving as a backdrop. Pete and I sat down first, and then Kate crawled onto her dad's lap, and Jack crawled onto mine—our family's natural divvy up. I heard Alan in my head: *Leave room on your lap so a birth mom can imagine her baby there.* I slid Jack off my lap, placing his little bottom onto the rock wall. I could tell he wanted to crawl back onto my lap, but I didn't *explain* anything to him; I just kind of stiff-armed him until he got the message. I felt horrible. But I looked warmly into the camera and smiled. (We could use none of those photos. I was basically giving Jack the Heisman in every shot.).

Photos done, it was time to write. Alan had shown us a few examples in his office, from a distance—not close enough to read the words but to get an idea of photos used, paper choices, etc. I saw a lot of stationery with watercolor, cuddly animals. One DBML was bound with raffia ribbon. I hoped those DBMLs were from the 90s.

No, that's not true. I hoped those were the DBMLs I'd be competing with.

Alan told us that getting the DBML to a final draft was a time-consuming project that would most certainly take many drafts on our part. He'd only accepted a first draft as the final draft once, and that adoptive father had been a Hollywood screenwriter.

I Googled: 'examples of Dear Birth Mom Letters.' Most hadn't been edited and had obvious grammar issues. One began, "We know this must be a difficult time in you're life." I wanted to see the best of the best—the DBMLs of families that had been *chosen*. During our consultation, Alan mentioned the 'Adoptive Families Gallery,' an area on his website where he posted his clients' DBMLs. Once ours was approved, and we paid an additional $1595 for six months of exposure, we could be posted in the 'Adoptive Families Gallery.' *There!* There, I'd be able to read DBMLs that'd received Alan's stamp of approval.

The 'Adoptive Families Gallery' was a freakin' *goldmine*.

Pam & Jeff: She was a cheerfully chubby mom-type, wearing a red cardigan and a cloth necklace made of little Mexican worry dolls. She looked bright and sunny and like her boobs would be the perfect pillow to lie on during a bedtime story. Jeff was balding, his face affable as he smiled out from under the hood of an old Pontiac with a just-right grease smudge on his cheek. Their letter was real, warm, and inviting. Best of all, under their name, it read: "Successfully Matched!" I read and re-read their DBML to catch their tone.

Elyn & Risa: An Asian lesbian couple. They described the garden in the backyard where their child would learn to grow things. (Shit, should we plant a garden?) They talked about the treehouse in their magical backyard. They described the reading corner with twinkly white lights and named a few of their favorite books that sat waiting on the shelves (Shit, why didn't I think of naming books I love? Books are my *thing*.).

Gary & Trina: Trina was a well-manicured, petite brunette with a high-powered job and a forced smile. Gary's gaze was vacant and he had a dated hairstyle (think Dan Quayle-ish) They had two boys, about five and seven, pressed and proper in matching outfits. In one photo, they were all in pajamas, lined up in Mom and Dad's bed, a big, loopy, "Grow old with me, the best is yet to be!" applique on the sky-blue wall above the headboard. Their DBML sounded too perfect; none of it rang true. I didn't take notes on Gary and Trina's letter.

I checked the 'Adoptive Families Gallery' multiple times a day. If one of the couples had been marked 'Successfully Matched!' the rest of my day was lopsided with jealousy. If there were no new matches, I felt a deep sense of schadenfreude; no one had risen above us! 'Matched' is the word used when a birth mom chooses adoptive parents for her baby. Being matched is the Holy Grail of domestic adoption. When prospective adoptive parents get together, common phrases are: *Have you been matched? When were you matched? How long was it between being matched and getting your baby? We were matched but it didn't work out.*

I sat down to write our DBML the last week of May. Jack was five and in half-day kindergarten and Kate was almost three and at preschool two mornings a week. As I sat in our office off the family room, I completely ignored the kids I had, to focus on writing about what a good mother I was. Jack and Kate enjoyed a steady stream of Chuggington and Doc McStuffins and "Help yourself to the snack bucket!" as I feverishly typed and edited. The irony wasn't lost on me, but I chalked it up to being, 'The best thing for our family in the long run.'

Part of the letter was to be written from Pete's perspective, in which he talked about me as a partner and as a mom. In our family, he's all things math/spatial/technological, and I'm all things written/family/social, so I asked Pete if he wanted me to write about how he felt about me, to which he responded, "Sounds good." So, I had a legit reason to interview my husband about what first drew him to me and what he loved about me. We'd been married for almost five years and communicated the things that pissed us off more than we shared the things that we appreciated about each other. But of when we first met, Pete told me:

"I liked the way you made other people feel comfortable and at ease, people we worked with, my family. I thought you were beautiful. And fun. I liked your sense of humor—that it was bawdy. And you were hot."

We had sex that night.

I found it easy to write about Pete, what I admired about him. The way he always did the right thing. The way I'd known he'd be a great dad—knew it to my core. How he loved his mom but not in an apron-strings way. It was also easy to write about our kids and their personalities, our home, and our community. The parts I wrestled with were our religious stance, and what we wanted our open adoption to look like.

I'm an atheist. Pete wouldn't check that box; he was raised Catholic. We don't attend church, teach our kids about any single god, or to have faith in a religious context. But I didn't want to include the word atheist in our Dear Birth Mom Letter. It sounded cold and cynical, of which we were neither. I called Alan. He said birth moms had a range of requests when it came to religion: They wanted a Christian family, or they wanted their child to be raised in a religion, but they didn't care which one, or they didn't want their child to be raised Catholic, or they didn't care about religious beliefs at all. Ultimately, I decided to leave religion out of the letter. It felt truer to let her see who we were by describing our life.

Finally, how to convey the level of openness we wanted? Full honesty would've been: *I want you to give us your baby and never want any contact with us outside of pictures and letters that can be exchanged via attorneys, so even that doesn't get too personal. I want to be the only one who comes within a million miles of being this baby's mom.* But I couldn't say that. And I wanted to be a better version of myself anyway.

Considering what we wanted our open adoption to look like and having to put it into words was a time of self-examination and ambivalence, being both prospective adoptive mom and adoptee. As an adoptive mom, I didn't want much contact with the birth mom. I was scared of the interpersonal messiness, the unwanted intrusions. But as an adoptee, I knew our child would probably want to know things about, have pictures of, or even meet their birth mom one day, and I wanted to give him or her an easy path to do that.

I couldn't find the words to say: *We-welcome-you-into-our-life-but-we-kinda-hope-you-want-your-privacy-too,* so I stole them. Remember Pam & Jeff, red cardigan/grease smudge? They'd said it perfectly, so I plagiarized these two sentences from their DBML: "We'd be happy to provide you with reassurance, updates, and photos if that is what you want. We want this child to know as much about you as you are comfortable sharing, your personality, likes, and interests, but the two of us also want to respect your privacy."

Dear Pam & Jeff,

If you're reading this, I apologize for plagiarizing your DBML. It was the first (and last) time I've ever done so, and I'm embarrassed. I can only hope that you take it as flattery and remember the sheer terror of writing the DBML as a shared experience between us.

Sincerely,
Denise

I sent my first draft off to Alan and wondered if, during future adoption consultations, he might now have to say that *only two special people* had nailed it on the first try.

It came back, as Alan called it, "a sea of red."

He hoped I wasn't discouraged, saying that the changes were "very minor" and that the second draft "should be the final." Disheartened, I looked through his edits. Most were for things like removing information that was too specific, like our city. He'd also crossed out anywhere I'd used 'love' in a frivolous way—nine times in just four pages.

"You can't say Pete 'loves' the Dallas Cowboys and then tell her you will 'love' her baby," Alan wrote. "It loses its meaning."

6

There were two books that never left my nightstand during our search: *Adoption in America: How to Adopt Within One Year*, by Randall B. Hicks, and, *Beating the Adoption Odds*, by Cynthia D. Martin and Martin Groves. Reading these 'how to find a baby fast' guides, I started to lose confidence in Alan. He'd sent us faded handouts on how to place a classified ad in the Thrifty Nickle and the USA Classified Network, which I'd never even heard of. Every hopeful adoptive parent who's seen *Juno* fantasizes about being found by a sweet, young girl flipping through the Penny Saver, but our nieces, ages sixteen to twenty, had all stayed with us in the past year, and they weren't reading classifieds; they were on Facebook, Instagram, and Vine. I had the foreboding feeling that Alan was VHS while other lawyers out there were digital, and we would be left in the dust.

Hicks recommended creating a one-page photo resume and getting it in the hands of people who might know of a girl. Examples of highly prized contacts were: high school/college counselors, hairstylists, clergy, and ob-gyns. It felt too intrusive, at first, asking friends to talk to their vagina doctor on my behalf. But when I called Dr. Chu to ask if I could send her a couple of our resumes, I found my motivation. Her response was short, direct, and intoxicating:

"Yeah. Off the top of my head, I know of two patients who aren't keeping their babies. I'll give them your letter. Send me several."

7

Alan called to say that our DBML was finalized, and he'd already FedExed a few copies to an adoption attorney in Central California, a colleague of his named Don. If Don didn't happen to be representing a couple with the attributes his birth mom was asking for, he'd call Alan and say something like: "Do you have a rural, horse-loving couple with a stay-at-home mom?" Like adoptive parent Go Fish. I wasn't too excited—I figured Don drew from Alan's pool of clients a couple of times a year at best, but then Alan said, "Don has matched five of my couples in the last month."

Five?! In the last month?! That *was* something to get excited about. I thanked Alan profusely as we said our goodbyes.

I greeted the other moms at school pick-up—normally a strictly in-and-out operation—with a, "Hey, *you*!" I magnanimously waved cars into traffic with a love-the-world smile. A lawyer we didn't even know was showing our DBML to pregnant girls in Central California *right now*. And this mystery lawyer, this Don, had made five matches with Alan's couples in the last month!

Central California was booming with babies. It felt like we might be next.

8

Pete and I met when I interviewed for an opening on his sales team. He was living in Hermosa Beach as a regional sales manager for a textbook company, and I'd just finished up my graduate program in English literature at Central Washington University.

I stood on the curb at the Ontario, California airport, the heat rising into my lined, woolen pantlegs. I'd told my prospective boss to look for the tall girl in a pinstriped suit. The way the sun hit the windshield, I couldn't make out his face when he pulled up in an inky-blue Chrysler 300. You know how they say women are chemically attracted to men who'll produce strong offspring? When Pete came around to put my bag in the trunk, all baby-making impulses were firing. *How am I gonna get through this interview?* I needed the job.

Using my professional voice, the one where I try to 'project from my diaphragm,' I extended my hand, "Nice to meet you in person," I said. "Thanks for picking me up."

I hoped my cheap-ass, oversized sunglasses didn't have scratches or crumbs nested in the frames.

"Thanks for making the trip," he said with a grin, taking my bag and putting it in his trunk.

I could taste his voice; it was like biting into a stack of Ritz crackers, crunchy and buttery at the same time. *Is that strawberry blonde? Our kids would be redheads.*

We'd kept it flirty but professional for almost a year when Pete invited me out to celebrate a big textbook sale I'd closed at Cal State San Bernardino. But he took me to the Sky Bar on

Sunset, which let me know it wasn't really a work dinner, and I'd hid a blue JanSport backpack in the back of my Jeep that held a toothbrush and a single make-up remover cloth, hoping it wasn't. We ended the night at his apartment in Santa Monica, where he read to me from the memoir his grandma had written.

"Would it be weird?" he asked.

"Would what be weird?" I said.

"If I kissed you?"

We moved from our first tentative kiss on his canvas slip-covered couch to fucking on his high bed with a stale-smelling, chambray duvet in less than a minute. The next morning, we wandered the pier and Ocean Avenue, settling in on the front porch of The Georgian, eating French toast dusted with powdered sugar and dripping with maple syrup and candied pecans.

He bought a bed for my cat, Tux, at his apartment, and I lay naked in bed with him for an entire Saturday trying to get into the NFL draft. Six months later, we'd moved into a Spanish-style apartment in Belmont Shore, and I was pregnant with Jack. We were content beyond anything either of us had ever known—floating in a bubble, breathing the rarified air of the newly in love and the first-time pregnant.

We were married in July of 2009, in a small ceremony in Santa Barbara. A soft, acoustic version of The Rolling Stones' *Wild Horses* carried me and my dad down the red dirt aisle. Jack, by then fourteen months, sat on Mom's lap and clapped when we kissed. We danced to Ray Lamontagne for our first song, and then later, after the vodka ran out and shoes came off, to *Apple Bottom Jeans*. We watched, feeling unbelievably lucky, as everyone we loved took a turn on the dance floor with Jack in their arms.

But there were fissures. We'd been living together for nearly two years, and we'd noticed things. Pete noticed I didn't keep the house as tidy as he liked, and my idea of cooking wasn't his. I noticed he wasn't as warm and welcoming to my family as he'd been in the beginning. I could be jealous. He could be stubborn.

I was staying home with Jack and knew Pete appreciated me, but I was accustomed to Real Recognition. I'd been the top seller at McGraw-Hill. They'd wanted me to move to New York before I stepped off the track and started walking around our apartment in a nursing bra, 24/7. It made me anxious to hear of colleagues being promoted beyond where I'd jumped off the track. I wanted back in.

We agreed on Dubuque, Iowa, because there were positions for both of us. Pete had lived in Chicago from age eleven to twenty-nine and warned me that I probably wouldn't like (would probably hate) the Midwest. But I was laser-focused on climbing the ladder, and if a two-year stint in the Midwest was what it would to take, then that's what we were going to do.

Standing under the stuccoed archway, our front door open to the scent of tuberose and the jacaranda that had bloomed the week we brought Jack home, Pete said, "I don't want to go. I'm happy here."

"Happiness can be found anywhere!" I said, in my don't-be-silly voice. "It's up to us to make our own happiness."

I hated Dubuque on sight.

The Iowa colors I'd seen in my head were green corn fields, red barns, and white picket fences. What I saw as we drove around Dubuque was a grey, depressed town. The Mississippi River and her waterfront were brown and muddy brown. On Main Street, every other storefront was vacant; the few open businesses mostly bars. My Smucker's commercial vision of

Iowa was replaced with the reality of U.S. Route 20, the main thoroughfare through town, bordered by gas stations advertising 'breakfast pizza,' drab strip malls, and an All-You-Can-Eat Chinese buffet in the shape of a Mayan Pyramid.

After a day of looking at houses, we stopped at Red Robin and took a booth in the bar. "Why are you crying?" Pete asked. "You don't like it here?"

All I had to do was nod. But it was too horrible to admit. I'd demanded that we uproot our life and move to Bumfuck, Iowa, and now I couldn't stand the sight of the place. He'd given his two weeks. We'd signed our contracts.

"I don't hate it here," I said. "It's just all so overwhelming."

"It'll be okay," he said, reaching across the table and grabbing my hands. "It's gonna be a great adventure for our family."

In our first winter, temperatures hit an all-time low of -37 degrees. My nose hairs froze into daggers as I walked the fifty yards from my car to the office. I became familiar with the term 'remote starter' and asked for one for Christmas. A very kind police officer pushed me home one afternoon, the nose of his patrol car on the butt of my Isuzu Rodeo, when I couldn't get enough traction to make it up the hill to the house we were renting (I didn't know about sandbags yet.). Leaving a prenatal appointment, I was T-boned by a teenager who slid into my driver's side door with his Toyota pick-up.

It wasn't just the weather. I wanted to tell Mari and Marcia about Dubuque, to laugh, to rage, but they were in California and some conversations require shared alcohol and facial expressions. (Mari and I had found each other on the cruise ship. She danced, enchanting audiences in crystal-encrusted costumes; I ran shuffleboard, trivia, and old-time sing-along in a navy polo and sensible white pumps.) The spin instructor played reggae. Everyone had taken the same vacation, someplace called The Dells. The people we worked with were smart and kind and tried to include us, but we didn't belong there. I didn't want to. I wanted to go home.

I should've said to Pete, "I one hundred percent fucked up our lives by moving us here. I'm sorry. You were right, and I was wrong. We're beach people. Can we go back to sandy weekends with our baby? Do you love me enough to know this is my fault but still help dig us out of this mess?"

Instead, I said none of that and made Pete the target of my contempt for Iowa: *he* was keeping us there. Pete was—rightly—resentful that he'd compromised, moved for my career and was repaid not with gratefulness but with bitterness. We traveled a lot for work. From January to May, we leapfrogged each other: he out one week, me the next. The travel kept us courteous, but the weekends were a herky-jerky, no-lube reentry into marriage. We got used to doing things our own way, and meeting someone else's expectations was a hassle.

Life wasn't awful, as Pete would point out. We had each other, good jobs, our healthy, happy little boy, our new baby girl, and we'd just bought our first home—a creamy yellow Cape Cod with a sledding hill and original hardwood floors. But as we went through the motions of planting roots, I had one foot on a flight home. Pete didn't love Dubuque or even like it a lot, but he thought it was okay and a good place to raise kids. That's one of the reasons I was first drawn to him—he's steady, takes things as they come. I don't. I feel strongly about things like people, places, and which table we're seated at in a restaurant, and if I don't like something, I feel the need to change it. *Now.* So, we lived with the tension of "I want to go home" vs. "It's okay here" for a year and a half. But one evening in March, Pete hit black ice and his Audi slid into a steep ditch with both kids in the car. Other cars were careening into the ditch, and it wasn't safe for them to stay where they were.

"Don't freak out, everyone's fine," Pete said, calling me at home. "But we slid into the ditch on Brunskill. We're gonna start walking; start driving and meet us."

When I saw them, my headlights illuminated the snow falling between us. Pete's strides were single-minded as he pushed through thigh-high snow with Kate—so small she was still in a bucket car seat—hooked in one arm, and two-year-old Jack clutched in the other.

We were back in California by the fall.

Dear Reader,

It has been pointed out to me that I sound like an asshole in this chapter. That my wrath against Iowa will alienate the entire Midwest. So, let me say, yes, of course, Iowa was beautiful. The green cornfields, the red barns, the white picket fences—they were all there. So were long afternoon walks with newborn Kate pressed to my chest, our sweat mingling as we made the Grandview loop, both of us lulled by the buzz of the cicadas. Iowa was lovely. I just couldn't see it. I was California's girl, and no one else was gettin' a shot.

Love,
Denise

9

I knew Facebook would be part of our marketing effort; I was on it all the time, anyway. But I was scared. Facebook was where I posted anecdotes and photos I'd chosen carefully to craft and maintain my public image: fun, adventurous, devoted mom, interesting, observant. And our family's public image: loving, active, down-to-earth, let's face it: *adorable*. Facebook wasn't a place where I posted vulnerabilities. I pitied people who did. We'd told family and close friends we were adopting, but posting to Facebook would be officially telling the world we wanted a baby and needed help finding one.

We needed a website, and Pete (all things tech) was on the road a lot, so I made our website using Weebly. I included a slideshow with the pictures I wanted a potential birth mom to see, set to Israel "IZ" Kamakawiwo'ole's mash-up of 'Somewhere Over the Rainbow' and 'Wonderful World.'

My first job out of college was working as cruise staff for Holland America. We ran the onboard activities: shuffleboard, golf chipping, karaoke, etc. Holland America was one of the more luxurious cruise lines, so the clientele was older. When a passenger had a heart attack or similar catastrophic medical event, the ship's officers would announce a 'Bright Star' over the loudspeaker to summon the medical staff: *"Bright Star in the Stuyvesant Lounge."* While the crew knew that someone was likely biting it, the passengers were blissfully unaware (unless they were in the Stuyvesant Lounge). One night, my boyfriend—Joey, the DJ—walked into his cabin where I'd been waiting for him.

"A guy died tonight in The Crow's Nest," he said.

I'd gotten off early and headed straight down to crew deck, where we could wear our regular clothes, smoke, and passengers weren't allowed, so I hadn't heard the Bright Star.

"I was playing Louis Armstrong's *Wonderful World* when the guy fell out," Joey said, throwing his navy blazer over the chair and walking toward me on his bed.

"That's a pretty good song to die to," I said, scooting over.

With the website done, I turned my attention to the text for my Facebook post. It couldn't be a vague, "Pete and I are hoping to find a birth mom; can you help us?" It had to have a *call to action*. So I wrote this:

July 23, 2013
Dear Facebook friends,

Pete and I have decided to add to our family through adoption. We could not be more excited! We are working through a great adoption attorney here in California, and he said that we can sit back and wait to be matched with a birthmother by him, or we can actively look ourselves. So, we are asking for your help in finding our son or daughter. There are two specific ways that you can help:
1. Will you please share this post on your page, saying that you know us personally and that we are hoping to adopt?
2. If you know of a woman who has decided to give her baby up for adoption and is looking for a loving and stable home, will you please give her our contact info? The link to our website is below, and it has all of our contact information as well as more information about who we are.

Posting something this intimate on fb feels a little vulnerable, but we are tossing caution aside because we're looking for our son or daughter. Thank you for your help and for joining us on this journey!

Denise & Pete

But even after I'd written what I wanted to say, I hesitated to post it. I was worried about the reactions of people who knew me professionally. I'd worked my ass off in Dubuque, earning a reputation as a woman who was *competent*. During a yearly review, my boss, Michelle, said, "You're the definition of urgency. I never worry about you getting shit done." Five years later, I was still lingering in the warmth of her praise. It was also important to me that people saw my family life as *enviable*. I had a handsome and loving husband; we had a boy and then a girl. Check, check, and check.

Telling the world I wanted a baby was the opposite of having it all. I would be telling friends I wanted something desperately and begging for their help. Posting on Facebook also meant that people would be keeping tabs on us; they'd know if we struggled to be matched—if it took years to find our baby. What if we were *never* chosen? If we failed, I'd never be able to post enough "fulfilled mommy" photos to convince people I was okay.

Pete had none of these reservations. For the 8,451 hours of thought I'd given to crafting the just-right Facebook post and wrestling with my fears of posting, he gave it less than a second's thought, and said: "Yeah, we should do that." If we'd discussed my fears of posting, which we never did except in my head, this is how the conversation would've gone:

Me: "I'm afraid to post this because I want to keep my (perceived) shiny, perfect reputation as someone who doesn't need help in life, especially with something as private as adding a child to our family. I'm worried about what Brian and Marty and Cindy will think—that they'll see me as *just a mom* and not a sales killer anymore. And not just a mom, but worse: *a needy mom*."

Pete: "Who gives a shit what they think?"

The night before I posted on Facebook, I went through and liked or commented on every single one of my friend's posts. I wanted them to be in a charitable place with me. You know how you give a 'like' to someone after they have 'liked' something of yours—like a thank you 'like'? It was that, but preemptive.

I researched the highest traffic time on Facebook; it was mid-afternoon on Tuesdays. So, on Tuesday, July 23, at 11:38 am Pacific (I posted mid-afternoon Eastern, to hit the maximum amount of mid-afternoon activity, nationally.), Pete sat at his desk with our laptop before him; I stood on his left holding his hand. There was no retrieving our privacy after this. My palms were sweaty, and my hands were shaking when I reached across Pete and hit 'Post.'

I tried to walk away and unload the dishwasher before checking for comments; I lasted about two plates and a bowl. Then I just sat down and watched the comments roll in. The response was overwhelmingly loving, supportive, and encouraging (and from a marketing standpoint, on message!). As people shared our post, they added personal stories about us as parents and people; waves of shared history, familiarity, and affection washed over me as I cried and scrolled. By 10 p.m., there were over forty comments of love and support, over forty people had shared our post, and our website had been visited 952 times.

Here's the math I did in my head: I had about 500 friends, so right off the bat, 500 people saw that we were trying to adopt and had the means to get ahold of us if they knew of any leads. Plus, forty friends shared our website on *their* page, and the average Facebook user had about 200 friends (though some of our college-aged nieces had over 1000). That meant that in that single day, potentially 8500 people learned about us via Facebook. Seeds were planted. Even if no one knew of a woman who was considering adoption *now*, they might hear of someone in the next few months.

The opposite of what I was afraid of happening happened. Instead of being seen as needy and desperate (If we'd gotten only a few shares or comments, I would've been paralyzed by rejection.), our family, friends, and even acquaintances made us feel worthy of a baby and brave for trying. The people who included personal comments were friends from every corner of my life: grade school, high school, freshman year dorm, old neighbors, the kids' daycare, sales reps I'd worked with, the gym, and so on. You know that one fantasy you have where you die, but you get to sit in on your own funeral like a ghost and just soak up everyone talking about how wonderful you were? It was like that.

Six days later, our website had received 2241 hits. In my 'how our adoption might go' fantasies, I expected that once we posted to Facebook—and *definitely* once I saw that we had 2241 hits—someone would call us saying, "I know of a girl…"

No one did.

10

In addition to Facebook, I'd heard of couples using Craigslist to find a birth mom. The idea being that you put an ad out there that said, "Hi, we're Pete and Denise and we're hoping to adopt a newborn," and a woman who was considering adoption happened upon your ad. The whole thing seemed sketchy, so I Googled: "Using Craigslist to find birth moms," and an article popped up from ABCnews.com, *Baby Wanted: Desperate Couple Advertise for Children on Craigslist.* Embedded in the article was a *Nightline* segment about the same couple, anchored by Cynthia McFadden (With McFadden opening by telling viewers that she herself was adopted). The article featured a picture of Dan and Tracey Citron of Michigan, standing with their beautiful and friendly-looking family and their son's birth mom. Their home was beautiful—I scrutinized the artwork on their walls, the quality of their furniture, the paint color they'd chosen for their family room. Their house was way nicer than ours. Maybe advertising on Craigslist didn't have to feel skeezy and dirty.

The article read:

"The Citrons went above and beyond to try to advertise themselves as prospective parents. They designed their own website, got their own 800 number for potential birth mothers to call, and even plastered their car with a personal ad. But after spending so much time, energy, and money, they said, nothing seemed to work. So they decided to try something different and turned to Craigslist. Tracey said she would start every morning by having a cup of coffee and placing her ad online. After about six weeks, she said she got a call on a June day, her birthday, from Tammy Nelson. She was looking for a way out. "When I Googled it, I put adoption in Phoenix, and the first thing to pop up was a Craigslist ad for Dan and Tracey. It was literally that quick," Nelson said. "I said, 'Hi, I'm pregnant, and I need help and this is the situation, what do you think?' And Tracey said, 'I'm really happy you called us.' It was perfect."

The way Tracey had spoken to Tammy? I couldn't imagine calmly greeting a birth mom that way. But there Tracey stood, beaming, her baby in her arms and her son's birth mom at her side.

The article went on to talk about the self-marketing Dan and Tracey had done. Tracey talked about how she'd designed the DBML, the website, and their business cards in the same style so they presented a consistent brand to birth moms who might be checking them out. *Consistent brand?* Tracey Citron was my Mother Ship.

There was a photo of their business card, a wide-trunked, flowering tree with a fresh, green background. It was gender-neutral and conveyed strength and roots. It was brilliant. Their 800 number was on the card. *Wait...can I call this woman and talk to her? There's no way the number will still work. They probably got their baby and ecstatically disconnected their 800 number the next day.*

Tracey picked up on the second ring.

"Hello?"

"Hi!" I said, feeling like someone had just shoved me onstage, "Um, this might sound kind of weird, but my name is Denise Massar and I'm a mom in Southern California. We're hoping to adopt, and I saw your story online and was wondering if I could ask you a few questions about your search? I hope it's okay I called—your number was on the card."

"Not weird at all; I'm happy to help," Tracey said.

"Thank you! That's so nice of you. Thank you," I said. "Okay, so I looked at Craigslist and was wondering, *where* in Craigslist did you post, like, under what category? And how'd you pick which towns you advertised in?" (The option of virtually every town/city in the United States had been daunting.)

"I posted under community," Tracey said. "And we posted in college towns, Austin, Tucson, Phoenix."

Of course.

I asked her about her business cards. She said a young woman named Heatherlee, a college student and designer at her husband's printing business, had created the design.

"She's *great*," Tracey said.

"Would you be willing to share her contact info with me?" I asked, aware that I was pushing the bounds of generosity and mentorship by a total stranger but willing to push until she pushed back if it helped me get her results.

"Sure," Tracey said, giving me Heatherlee's number. "I'm not sure if she's still doing side jobs, but give it a shot."

One of the things that drew me to Tracey was her businesslike approach to finding a birth mom. There was no weepy blogging; there was a fully formulated and executed marketing plan.

In the Nightline segment, as Tracey and Dan strolled through their expansive, manicured backyard, Tracey said to the interviewer "You don't wait for a job, you look for a job. So why would you wait for a baby?" I loved her style—it was my style. No, it was my style's more- polished big sister.

The conversation with Tracey was pivotal for me. She had put it all out there. She'd asked for a baby on Craigslist. She'd driven around with a vinyl decal on the back window of her car that read: "We are hoping to grow our family through adoption, call us at 1-800-xxx-xxxx," for god's sake. And yet nothing about her spoke of desperation. Yes—she had her baby in her arms by the time I spoke with her, but even if she'd still been searching, there was nothing desperate about Tracey. She'd been a woman with a goal: to find a baby to love. And she'd approached it the way she'd approach a professional goal, strategically and methodically. I found a role model in Tracey. I began seeing my search not as desperate, but as someplace I could kick ass. I was strategic and methodical at work; I'd be the same in our search. I liked to win. And winning your adoption search meant you ended up with a baby in your arms.

11

Pete posted to Facebook a week after I did, and less than twenty-four hours later, he walked into the den where I was watching *Parenthood* and polishing off a bag of dried mango and said, "My friend Gina Piacenza sent me a message about a baby."

"*What?*" I answered, jumping up from the couch and scrambling over the ottoman.

"Yeah," he said, the laptop balanced in the crook of his arm, his face glowing blue. "She said she knows about a baby through a friend and wants to know if we're interested."

"Who's Gina again?" I asked as I grabbed the computer and expanded her message.

Gina was the sister of one of Pete's best friends growing up. Pete and Steve had been part of the same pack that roamed Highland Park and Gina was still close with Pete's sister, Mary.

Highland Park was that kind of town.

Gina's message said she'd received a call from a friend a couple of days ago asking if she was interested in adopting a baby. She replied that she and her husband weren't in a position to adopt right now, and then she'd seen Pete's post on Facebook.

We messaged Gina back that, yes, we were *very interested* in adopting the baby and could be in Chicago with a moment's notice.

When you're searching for a baby to adopt and someone tells you they've just been offered a baby—unsolicited—that becomes, hands down, the most fantastical story you've ever heard.

I messaged Gina: W*here did your friend find this baby?*

This is how it went down:

An inner-city Chicago nurse came into contact with a patient who wanted to place her baby for adoption.

The nurse called a woman named Ann, whom she'd called before. Ann and her husband had adopted three babies and all three adoptions had started this way, with a call from this nurse saying a baby was available.

This time, when the nurse called, Ann and her husband said that their family was complete.

But Ann had a friend named Teresa who might want to adopt the baby, so she gave her a call. Teresa said that she and her husband weren't in a place to adopt, but that her friend, Gina, might be. So, Teresa called Gina.

Gina and her husband had already adopted a son, and they were on a waitlist for a baby girl from China when they got the call from Teresa. They told her they didn't want to adopt the baby, but Gina, having just seen Pete's Facebook post, told Teresa she might know of a family.

Gina then messaged Pete while I sat on the sofa eating dried mangoes and watching *Parenthood*.

Gina wrote, "My friends just keep getting these calls for newborns from a nurse who works at the hospital. I don't know if that is allowed, so we'll keep that part a secret." She said the nurse had told Ann the baby was due in a month, and the mother likely hadn't had any prenatal care. Ann thought the baby was most likely Black because the three babies she'd adopted, and learned about through this nurse, were Black.

Hold up. There was a nurse who, on a regular basis, came into contact with ready-to-pop women who weren't keeping their babies but hadn't chosen adoptive parents yet? I wanted to get on *that* nurse's call list; I wanted to be at the tippy top of that freakin' list. *And, hell yes, Gina!* Your secret's safe with me.

In the last message Gina and I exchanged that night, she said Ann had contacted another couple after she'd passed on adopting the baby. She said she'd reach out to Ann in the morning to find out what the other couple had said.

Lying in bed that night, I started to feel like this might be our baby. And I felt like it was a girl. The way she'd been brought to us was like the stories I'd read in the adoption books. It was never a clean, linear line when people found their babies; it was always a somebody who knew somebody's sister story—*just like this*. I thought about the puffy, lightest-of-pink sleeper I'd bundle her in at the hospital. Were we going to skip right over all of the crazy encounters with potential birth moms—the awkward and heartbreaking contact Jennifer Gilmore had documented so well in *The Mothers*—to just hop on an SNA to ORD flight and go get our baby girl?

That the mom had had no prenatal care didn't faze us—it wasn't one of our deal breakers. Our deal breakers were alcohol or drug use by the birth mom (we were fine with pot), or a family history of mental illness. That the baby was Black was exciting. I could see her little face; I could feel her hair. I was ready to prove that color didn't matter. I Googled, 'How to care for Black hair,' before I went to bed.

The next morning, there was a message from Gina:

Just got word the other family is moving forward. My friend will let me know if anything changes. I am sorry this didn't work out. Do trust though, your baby will come to you.

I was disappointed, but not devastated. It had all happened so quickly. I thought about Gina's words. She was an adoptive mom; she knew where we were at—she'd waited for her son, and now she was waiting for her daughter. Her offer of encouragement was kind, and I took it to heart.

But it was an odd feeling to let go of this baby who'd wisped through my mind for less than twelve hours. She wasn't gone from this world. If we'd been one higher in the message chain, she would've been ours.

12

In early August, I received a Facebook message from our friend, Lori. Lori was married to one of Pete's closest friends, Dean. She was smart and just the right amount of snarky. At the time of our wedding, Lori was going through chemo and had lost her hair. She wore a sun hat to the ceremony, but after the sun set, she danced, and drank, and held conversations bravely, beautifully, bald. She was a professor at De Paul University School of Nursing and had jokingly told me she hoped one of her high-achieving nursing students would get drunk and knocked up and we could have her baby. Lori's message read:

> I think this is an amazing thing you are doing! I wanted to connect you with my cousin Liz. They adopted their daughter in five months through private means, and she said she would be happy to help you if she can. Let me know if you need more information.

I snooped Liz on Facebook. She had one of those gregarious, dimpled smiles where you couldn't help but smile back. Thick waves of auburn hair fell past her shoulders. Her Facebook page was full of pictures of her daughter—the baby girl they'd found in just five months, who now looked to be about six years old, and was gorgeous and vivacious and so firmly *theirs*. I went to the website for Liz's interior design firm. She designed minimalistic, beachy, light-filled rooms that ended up in design magazines and won major awards.

On Sunday afternoon, I called Liz at her home on Martha's Vineyard. I'd scribbled two questions on my legal pad: *Self-marketing? Openness?*

Liz was warm and generous with her knowledge. I asked if they'd done their own marketing. She said they hadn't, that they'd hired an adoption facilitator. Liz explained that a facilitator was someone, usually a woman, who did the work of finding a birth mom for you. All of the self-marketing stuff that was time-consuming, vulnerable, and messy, a facilitator handled for a fee. A facilitator could find a birth mom for you, Liz said, but couldn't handle the legal aspects of an adoption; a lawyer was needed to see the adoption through. Facilitator = Matchmaker.

Hiring a facilitator sounded good for so many reasons. I'd been at it for a month and we still hadn't gotten any bites—Gina had contacted us about a baby, but a birth mom hadn't contacted us directly yet. And I'd become obsessed with self-marketing. It was taking time away from the kids, Pete, and our household, and I felt guilty for how the search had taken over—balls were definitely being dropped. And finally, though I'd gotten braver about begging people to help me find a baby, I still didn't *like* doing it. A facilitator would do the begging for me.

Liz said they'd worked with a facilitator at For Keeps Adoptions in Santa Monica, just 45 minutes north of us. Their facilitator's name was Carol and she'd been wonderful.

"There was never a day that we didn't get at least something encouraging about a potential birth mom from her," Liz said. "And we were matched within two weeks of signing with them."

Two weeks???!!!

Their first match hadn't worked out for some reason, but Carol had worked extra hard for them after the disappointment of a failed match.

"We were matched again in just a few weeks," said Liz. They had a few months to get to know their birth mom, and then they welcomed their daughter home.

I still couldn't imagine having a real conversation with a woman considering giving us her baby. Liz had talked to a real live birth mom. She'd had that first awkward conversation and the one after that. And she'd performed in a manner in which the birth mom still wanted to give Liz her baby.

"What do those conversations feel like? What do you talk about?" I asked Liz.

"All our early communication was through emails. Would you like to read them?" she asked.

"That would be amazing," I said. "If you're willing to share, I'll read every single word."

After Liz and I said goodbye, I thought about how knowing good people always leads you to other good people. I met and married Pete, Pete was friends with Dean, Dean had married Lori, and now Lori's cool cousin Liz was helping us find our baby. I had renewed energy and was full of hope. TWO WEEKS! I vowed to be like Liz after we had our baby. She was open with information, encouraging, and wanted to help us. She'd longed for a baby, too; she knew what it felt like. But she had her baby now. I couldn't wait to get to where she was.

As soon as Liz and I hung up, I called Carol at For Keeps. Liz and Kevan had been matched in two weeks, so if I hired Carol that day, I reasoned, we could have a baby in our arms by the end of summer. The woman who answered the phone said Carol was out (probably out getting a baby, I thought!) and wouldn't be in again until the next day. I made an appointment to speak with her the following afternoon.

That evening, Liz forwarded the emails she'd exchanged with her birth mom, Kat. I devoured them. It was the first time I heard a birth mom's actual voice and the first time I'd seen a model for what my voice could sound like as a prospective adoptive mom. Kat's emails were tentative at first: "I'm a little nervous, not really sure how we do this…," but later—the emails took place over a couple of weeks—Kat's voice got stronger as she told Liz and Kevan more about who she was and what kind of parents she was looking for. Kat was smart, articulate. She had a little girl already and loved her fiercely. She said she would love to keep her baby but knew what it took to raise a child financially and knew she couldn't do it. Liz's emails back to Kat were just *Liz*—her own bubbly voice, with an overuse of capitalization and exclamation marks for emphasis.

I'd imagined my future conversations with birth moms as being more subdued—this woman would be giving us her child—wouldn't she expect and deserve a reverence acknowledging the gravity of the situation? But reading Liz and Kat's emails, I saw the tone didn't need to be somber. Kat was sad that she couldn't find a way to raise her baby, but she was at peace with her decision to place her baby for adoption. And something else came through in the emails between Kat and Liz, something I'd never considered before: Kat was *happy* to have found Liz and Kevan. She said it gave her peace, with her due date looming less than one month away, that her baby would be loved and cared for. It was the first time I considered that our adoption might be reciprocal. That it didn't necessarily have to be me somehow finessing a woman into giving me her child and then running inside with the baby clutched to my chest, twisting and turning one thousand deadbolts, crossing my fingers and down on my knees, praying to a god I didn't believe in that we'd make it to finalization day before the birth mom realized, *of course*, that she'd made the biggest mistake of her life. Reading Kat's emails, I understood that a birth mom could be sure. That our adoption could be an agreement between two women who were certain. That there would be giving on both sides.

Carol's voice was friendly and efficient. I told her I'd talked to Liz and knew their For Keeps story—how wonderful she'd been to work with, how quickly she found birth moms.

Carol explained how she worked. Using the fees paid by prospective adoptive parents, she was able to buy internet advertising on a large scale. She could cast a very wide net, much farther than we'd be able to do on our own. She said that kind of large-scale advertising took time and money but paid off in a big way; rarely a day went by that a birth mom didn't contact her. I couldn't even imagine. Birth moms were like fish in a barrel for Carol.

"Part of what makes For Keeps unique is that we only work with fifty families at a time, so it's not like you'd be up against hundreds of families. You can start the application process right away," she said. They happened to have a couple of spots open.

It all sounded fantastic, but Liz had already sold me the day before. Carol didn't need to say a thing.

I asked her about the fees. That was going to be the hard part. We were already in for about $7500 with Alan's retainer, professional photos, and printing of the DBML and flyers. And the match fee, birth mom expenses, and finalization fees would (hopefully) need to be paid, and that'd be, roughly, another twenty grand. Pete didn't know I was calling Carol. He would've said there was no point because we weren't going to hire her. He would've said we'd only been looking a month—to *give it some time.*

For Keeps' fee was $9000. That would buy us their services for two years, no matter how many times we were matched. That was a big deal. When Alan matched us, we'd pay a fee of $5000, but if the match failed for any reason—even if the birth mom simply changed her mind—we'd be out that $5000 and have to pay it again the next time he matched us.

So, fear of a failed match was half the fear of getting our hearts crushed and half fear of draining our bank account and being too broke to try again. When Carol said they'd match us as many times as needed for a single fee, that was attractive. I thought maybe I could sell Pete on that.

She talked more about what our $9000 would get us, how they used special programs to ensure that For Keeps came up near the top in the Google searches by birth moms looking for adoptive parents. Possibly sensing our pocket depth from my tepid response, Carol offered:

"But if you're willing to adopt an African American baby, the fee is only $5000."

Did she just say that out loud? That Black babies are basically half-off?

She delivered the fee structure without embarrassment or apology—like she was reading a grocer's ad in the Sunday paper: strawberries $2.20, blueberries $3.99.

I hurried our goodbyes. We couldn't afford $9000. We couldn't afford $5000.

I couldn't stop thinking about what Carol had said. Why did Black babies cost less to adopt than white babies? Was it racism? Was it supply and demand? And didn't low demand equate to racism? And how, in 2016, were there organizations setting fees according to skin color? Maybe For Keeps was an anomaly, I thought. I started digging around.

I found an Illinois Times article that called out American Adoptions in Overland Park, Kansas, for setting fees based on the adoptable child's race. The article was written in 2005, so I figured after being exposed eleven years prior, American Adoptions would've changed their fee structure. The sales representative who answered the phone, Mike, broke it down for me:

"For the Traditional Program, the fees range from $33,500 to $50,000," he said.

If you enrolled in the Traditional Program, Mike explained, you would be adopting a baby that was white, any race other than African American, or any mix of races that didn't include African American.

"But fees for the Agency Assisted program," he said, "range anywhere from $26,500 to $40,000."

"What does Agency Assisted mean?" I asked.

"There's a greater need for families in that program, so the adoption cost that would go toward advertising and marketing to locate birth moms is a bit less," Mike said.

"I would love a Hispanic baby," I said. "Where would a Hispanic baby fall between the two programs?"

"A Hispanic baby would be in the Traditional Program," Mike said. "Any baby other than African American would be considered traditional."

"My husband would prefer a baby of mixed race, Hispanic and Black. Where would that fall?"

"That would be the Agency Assisted program," Mike said. "Any African American at all—even a quarter—that'll be Agency Assisted."

What Mike said was shocking. It also sounded vaguely familiar. Remember the one-drop rule? When plantation owners raped their African American slaves, children were produced, and whites started freaking out because it was getting harder and harder to tell at a glance who was Black and who was white. So, the one-drop rule—initiated in the South but soon accepted as the national standard—stated that any Negro blood, even "one drop," made a person a Negro and designated them as a second-class citizen. If you learned about the one-drop rule in high school in the '80s like I did, it'd seemed like ancient history. Pre-March on Washington. Pre-civil rights. Certainly, pre-election of Barack Obama. But here it was, 2016, and the one-drop rule was still around.

In 2013, NPR's Michele Norris founded The Race Card Project, in which she invited people to distill their thoughts on race into six words and send them to her via postcard. One listener sent in a postcard that read: "Black Babies Cost Less to Adopt." Shortly after, Michele met Minnesotan adoptive mom Caryn Lantz. Caryn, who was white, had recently adopted her son, who was Black, and told Michele about a conversation she and her husband had had with a representative from Heart to Heart Adoptions in Utah:

"And [she] was telling us about these different fee structures that they had based on the ethnic background of the child…the cost to adopt the Caucasian child was approximately

$35,000, plus some legal expenses. Versus when we got the first phone call about a little girl, a full African-American girl, it was about $18,000."

When I talked to Carol at For Keeps, I hadn't stumbled upon the one facilitator that was pricing their services according to a child's skin color. It was a known and accepted practice.

There is out in the open racism in day-to-day life in our country, like when our elderly neighbors were relieved to meet Pete and me when we moved in because they'd seen a Black man going in and out of our house (our realtor, Michael). And then there are versions of racism hidden in the nooks and crannies of our society that only a small slice of the population sees, like in private adoption where Black babies cost less to adopt than white babies.

13

We never knew when Alan was presenting us to birth moms. He'd explained during our initial consultation that he wouldn't let us know each time he presented us—that the emotional rollercoaster was too great. I half-heartedly agreed that that sounded like a good idea. We only knew we'd been presented to a birth mom when Alan's bill arrived at the end of each month. I've inserted these boxes, so you'll know—though Pete and I didn't—the days in which a birth mom received our DBML:

> 8/07/2013 DBML sent to Riley F.

> 8/08/2013 DBML sent to Jodi

Ripping open Alan's bill, I'd read the women's names while standing next to the mailbox. Even though they hadn't chosen us, it was still thrilling.

What were we doing on Tuesday, August 7? Normal work day, freelanced in the morning, and then maybe I cleaned the kitchen or a toilet before turning my mind to dinner. And a girl named Riley held our letter in her hands and considered giving us her baby.

Wednesday, August 8. The kids and I were at the Orange County fair. We petted the goats and the wallaby in the petting zoo; we paid a dollar to look at a sad crocodile behind Plexiglas; we ate shaved ice, and a woman named Jodi held our letter and wondered if I'd be a good mom.

14

By mid-August, I was fearless. Obsessive. I saw *eh-vah-ree-won* through the prism of: *How can this person be used to find a baby?* Meeting new people, I wondered how much polite chitchat was required before I brought up our search and handed them a flyer.

My spin instructor was a young woman named Whitney. Whitney was a civil litigation lawyer and a spin instructor on the side. We, her devoted class, had been with her through her taking and passing of the BAR and felt like a loose, cool kid's club. My M.O. was to sit in the second row, off-center left, and talk to no one. So, I knew the faces but none of the names. But now, I saw my spin class anew: a captive audience of fifty people. And people who came to 9:15 a.m. spin class on Saturday were doers.

One Saturday morning in mid-August, I brought in a Kinko's box heavy with flyers and a box of our business cards. I'd messaged Whitney asking if I could have the floor for two minutes before class, and she was happy to help.

"Hi. My name is Denise," I said, my voice shaking. I hoped it was minor and rationalized that no one knew what my normal voice sounded like anyway. "My husband and I are hoping to adopt a newborn through independent adoption. Our lawyer said we can sit back and wait for him to match us with a birth mom, or we can try to find one ourselves." My voice was shaking in a *for sure* noticeable way. I tried some hand gestures to convey casualness and stood a little taller. "Basically, that means that we're hoping to find a woman who's considering placing her baby for adoption, and I'm asking you guys for your help today." I scanned the room for smiles, encouraging nods. *Nothing.* "So…um…if you know a woman who's facing an unwanted pregnancy, would you please pass our flyer on to them? And even if you don't know of anyone right now, please take one of our business cards…in case you hear of anyone in the future." Desperate to get back to the safety of my bike, I chirped out, "Okay, well…thanks so much!" with a little wave and a shoulder shrug that I hoped said: *I know this whole thing sounds crazy, but please like me anyway.*

I went to my bike in the front row and tried not to make eye contact with anyone. I especially tried to act like I hadn't just asked them all to get me a baby. I was trying to clip my shoes into the pedals nonchalantly but couldn't because my legs were shaking so hard.

We spun and sweated, and class was over. I'd left my Kinko's box and business cards by the door so people could grab one on the way out. I watched, trying to act like I wasn't, to see who would take one, who was willing to help. I watched with an intensity equal to how I watch my kids in social situations when I suspect they're being bullied or otherwise excluded, which is to say, hyper-vigilantly and ready to hold an Eternal Grudge against anyone who mistreated them (or in this case, didn't take a flyer).

As people filed out, more than not bent over and grabbed a flyer and a few business cards. Even the men, which surprised me. I assumed that for most men my longing for a baby and my search for a pregnant woman in crisis would be too feminine, too emotional, too messy of a topic, and they'd take a pass.

As I wiped my bike down, a woman approached me, introducing herself as Barb. "I have a friend in Oceanside who helps people find babies to adopt," she said.

I asked Barb if her friend was a facilitator. She said she wasn't sure exactly what her friend did or how she found babies, but that I should give her a call. I fantasized that Barb's friend wasn't a facilitator who'd want $9000 but a nice old woman who found babies for free. In my head, I pictured Barb's friend as a bonneted Mother Goose.

"Her last name is Love," Barb said. I wondered if that was a sign.

She said she'd introduce us via Facebook message as soon as she got home, wished me good luck, and walked out the door.

A white-haired man with a kind face had been waiting just beyond Barb. He approached my handlebars and introduced himself as Bill.

"My wife and I adopted both of our kids, and it was the best decision we ever made," he said, his eyes glistening with emotion. His kids were grown now and had kids of their own. "I remember right where you're at, waiting for your baby," he said. He wished us the very best. I was deeply touched. Every time I saw Bill at the gym after that, he'd ask how the search was going.

I took off my bike shoes, threw them in my bag, and was switching to tennis shoes when a young woman came up and introduced herself as Kelly. She was an ER nurse at Hoag Hospital in Newport Beach.

"I'll take your flyer and put it up in our break room if you'd like. We're a tight-knit group," she said. "If you want to send it to me digitally, I'll ask my nurse friends around Orange County to print it off and post it in their break rooms, too."

I couldn't believe how much Kelly was willing to do for me; other than probably having sized each other up in class, we were total strangers. Yet she was extending all of this kindness toward me, going out of her way to help and was willing to ask her colleagues to help me, too.

"Oh, one more thing…," Kelly said as we walked out of the dark spin room, into the brightly-lit gym. "I work with a woman who's pregnant, a nurse, and she's not sure she wants to keep the baby. It was an unplanned pregnancy, she's just a couple months along, but she was telling me last week that she's considering adoption. I'll give her one of your flyers."

As Kelly and I said our goodbyes, I thanked her profusely. I was already assigning stock nurse characteristics to this mystery nurse: she was sensible, no-nonsense, science-minded, and if she decided to place her baby for adoption, she'd surely follow through with clinical detachment.

I went back into the spin room to gather up the nearly empty Kinko's box and remaining business cards. Whitney was storing away the mic. I thanked her for letting me talk to the class and for leading me to Barb, Bill, and Kelly. She took a flyer and said she'd pass it on to a colleague's father who was a big fertility doctor—maybe he'd have some connections.

The experience of speaking to my spin class was a reminder that people, on the whole, were overwhelmingly kind and willing to help. I'd shown vulnerability, and Barb, Bill, and Kelly had rewarded me with encouragement and practical help that was so wonderful, so *specific*, I couldn't have imagined asking for it myself. I was reeling. As soon as I got home, I would look up the Love lady on Facebook and find out what her deal was and how she found babies. I was going to send our digital flyer to Nurse Kelly, who was, in turn, going to post our flyer in hospital break rooms all over Orange County for a zillion nurses to see.

Pete and I met up to go get Jack and Kate out of Kid's Klub. The girls who worked there, ages eighteen to twenty-one and highly social, were some of my top networking priorities, and I'd planned to give each of them a flyer that day. Pete and I walked into Kid's Klub. Crocs and sandals made a rubbery, toe-jam-scented mound by the door; sippy cups of milk and snack cups of Cheerios lined the counter, and Sophia the First played on the TV. As Pete got Jack and Kate wrangled and into their shoes, I approached Bree. She was one of my favorites. A gentle, porcelain-skinned girl with a gorgeous mane of red curly hair, I'd watched her with Jack and Kate and seen that she favored them. I handed Bree a flyer, half-energy, "…so if you know of anyone, please pass this on." I was so high from Barb, Bill, and Kelly, I needed nothing from Bree. I just wanted to check "Girls in Kid's Klub" off of my networking spreadsheet.

"I love your photo. Sooooo cute!" Bree gushed as she looked at our flyer. "I'll tell all my friends about you—I *love* you guys." Then, moving her gum from one side of her mouth to the other, she said, "You know Roya? The girl that works the front desk? She's pregnant."

Did I know of the pregnant girl who worked the front desk? Yes. Yes, I did.

While we were searching, I was acutely aware of every pregnant woman who crossed my path. And I hated them. I hated them because they had what I desperately wanted, and because they had it, they could be nonchalant about it. They pushed grocery carts around Albertsons or chased their toddlers on the beach. When I saw a pregnant woman place her hand on her belly I—internally—rolled my eyes because, *my god, that move's a little showy isn't it?* Suspicious she'd patted her roundness as a one-upmanship directed at me, I'd make sure she didn't see *me* see *her* pat her belly, to let her know her catty message had not been received.

I saw a woman at the beach, about six months along. She was wearing a bikini in a perfect shade of green, a sage I'd been searching for for years. Her rounded belly, taut and brown, caught the late afternoon sunlight. I did the math. It would be a Christmas baby. The joy of a Christmas baby seemed excessive, almost gaudy. And there she was, plain-faced and bored, tossing buckets and shovels into a bag,

Ashley, a friend of a friend, was pregnant with a baby girl while we were searching. I liked Ashley; she was sweet, kind, a first-grade teacher. She'd waited a long time to find a partner and to have the baby I knew she'd always wanted. She deserved all of the happiness she could find. I watched her belly posts on Facebook: *5 months! 6 months! 7 months!* Around her due date, I started looking for a "She's here!" post but didn't see one. I wondered if something had gone wrong. I *hoped* it had. During that time, I always hoped that something would go wrong when friends, acquaintances, even celebrities delivered their babies. It didn't have anything to do with wishing harm on the babies; I wanted all babies to be healthy and safe. It had to do with the women. I wanted to steal their joy. If their joy could be squelched, my envy could be managed.

Ashley finally posted her daughter's arrival. There'd been complications. Her daughter had swallowed meconium and been air-lifted to another hospital immediately following the C-section. Mother and daughter were at separate hospitals, but everyone was doing great. I was happy. Happy that some of her joy had been stolen.

I answered Bree, "Hmmm…yeah, I think I know the girl you're talking about."

"Well, she's pregnant, and she doesn't want to keep the baby. I think the guy was a jerk. Her family really wants her to keep it, but she doesn't want to; I know that. I'll tell her about you guys."

Roya was Middle Eastern and gorgeous. Like Kardashian-gorgeous, but without all the lip-plumping and vapidness. She would make gorgeous babies. She *was* making a gorgeous baby. What if this was it? "Our birth mom actually turned out to be the girl who checked us in at the gym," we'd say. "Isn't that *crazy*?"

I told Bree I'd love it if she told Roya about us and thanked her. "You're the best," I said, meaning it, as I hugged her goodbye. Pete held Kate's hand and I held Jack's as we walked out the front door of the gym. I dropped into the passenger side of our Equinox, sweaty and spent.

Holy shit.

15

THE HOME STUDY

Alan gave us the name of an adoption agency that could complete the home study for us.

The woman who answered the phone at Lullaby Christian Adoptions introduced herself as Lynda. She had a saccharin-sweet older woman's voice, and I imagined her in smart taupe slacks, a floral blouse, and a pink cashmere cardigan draped over her shoulders. Lynda said she'd send us a welcome packet containing everything we needed to know about completing our home study. Their fee was $2500, she said. I put the check in the mail the same day, eager to get started.

The packet arrived a few days later, and I was deflated from the moment I scanned the thirty-item Home Study Checklist. The only silver lining I saw was that completing the checklist would take persistence, and I knew that some of my competition—other hopeful adoptive parents—wouldn't complete it as quickly as I would. Some never would.

I was anxious, approaching the home study. I'd have to get a physical, and I always went into doctor's exams fearing a cancer diagnosis. We would need to document exactly how much we were worth monetarily, and I intentionally kept that number vague in my head—was our savings an embarrassment for two people in midlife? A social worker would ask us: "What drugs have you used?" "Do you have a criminal record?" and "How's your marriage?" We'd be tested for HIV, which, as a child of the '80s, always evoked a flutter of fear in my heart, along with images of Tom Hank's cracked lips and the AIDS Quilt unfurled in front of Reagan's White House. I would need to provide health histories for Jack and Kate to prove that they hadn't been abused, which, even though the logic was clear, felt insulting. All of it was intrusive, but I saw the reasoning behind it—due diligence had to be paid to ensure babies were placed with appropriate and able parents.

The parts of the home study I found aggravating were the non-essential tasks, like: Floor Plan of Your Home (may be your own drawing!), and Confirmation of Completion of Required Reading. "Confirmation of Completion of Required Reading" was agency speak for book reports.

Book reports? Are you kidding me? I wanted to call the VP of Home Study Checklists and say, "I'll share details of our sexual compatibility and provide our bank statements; I'm kind of an over-sharer anyway. I'll tell you about the time I shoplifted a Quicksilver sweatshirt from The Bon at Capital Mall and got my period while mall security arrested me. You can poke through our cabinets. We'll take the two classes you require *and* pay you even more money to take said classes (funny how that works). But book reports? *You can go fuck your five fucking book reports.*"

But, of course, I did the book reports. Because I am a rule-follower and an ass-kisser.

And when you want a baby, you check every box.

16

One day in the middle of August, a woman named Eileen sent us an email:

Dear Denise,

On July 30th I had a baby girl. I cannot keep her, it's my choice. Actually, I can't bring myself to keep her. My decision is because she is a baby born from hate, not love. I was raped by two different men ... I know it's not her fault, but I can't bring myself to even look at her for fear of seeing those animals looking back at me, because one of them is the father. She is in foster care. The worst part is I didn't know I was pregnant. I was in such a bad depression, and I didn't eat or sleep much, and so I began to drink and use cocaine in the last three months of my pregnancy. Knowing she was positive for cocaine made me feel like dying. I was so ashamed and disgusted with myself. So, that's my story, and I just want her to be loved and to never feel ashamed or unwanted.

Eileen

I could do that, I thought. *Make sure this baby knows how loved she is, how wanted. I could make sure she never feels ashamed. Maybe this baby needs me more than any other baby in the whole world.*

August 16, 2013
Dear Eileen,

First of all, I am so sorry to hear about what happened to you. No one should ever have to experience that, and I am so sorry that you did. I hope the men are facing legal consequences for their actions. Where do you live? Do you have family or friends with you to support you during this time?
I look forward to hearing back from you.

Denise

August 17, 2013
Denise

I have a supporting family, but my parents are too old to raise her. My brother is single and my sister has three daughters of her own, so she financially can't raise her. I live in Las Cruces, New Mexico. I did not report the rape. I hid it out of Shame and fear.

Eileen

I wondered if she'd capitalized 'Shame' on purpose.
I sent her emails to Alan and gave him a call, excited to lay our first birth mom contact at his feet.
"The cocaine and alcohol use isn't good," he said.

This was seventh-grade health stuff—I could see Mrs. Overmeyer rolling out the AV cart. I knew it wasn't *good*. I knew there was no way to predict the long-term effects on the baby.

"But it hasn't *necessarily* affected the baby," I countered.

"You should talk to a trusted doctor about the effects of cocaine and alcohol on a fetus, or Google it even, then you and Pete can have an informed conversation about whether this is a baby you want to proceed with," he said. "Also, the fact that the baby is in foster care with CPS is not good. Once a child is placed in CPS, it can be very, very difficult to shake out."

I envisioned a baby caught up in brambles, Pete and I on our hands and knees in the dirt, trying to pull her from the twisted vines, her pink terrycloth sleeper snagging on the thorns.

"This birth mom opportunity is like a ham half-off," Alan said.

"What does that mean?" I asked him, having a vague idea but not a clear one, and I needed clarity.

"There is a woman coming to you wanting to give you her baby, but what is the quality of this opportunity?" he asked. "You'll have a long fight for a baby that is stuck in the foster system, and the baby could have serious delays and defects due to the mother's cocaine and alcohol use. Some would call this the Jewish dilemma—why would a ham be half off? An observant Jewish person would not eat non-kosher food like ham, regardless of the fact that it was on sale or half off the regular price."

I got off the phone with Alan thinking he'd picked a helluva time for an obscure idiom, but I understood his position, and I knew in my gut he was right. Our intention wasn't to save a drug baby; we wanted to add a healthy baby to our family. But still. The ultimate goal was to have a birth mom contact us and ask us to parent her baby, and Eileen had done that. I'd never imagined a scenario where we would say no.

I came in from the patio to find Pete in the kitchen, making a sandwich. I hadn't told him about Eileen yet; I knew what his answer would be and didn't want to hear it. We'd missed an opportunity with the Chicago baby, and I didn't want to lose another. I pulled up Eileen's email. While he read it, I leaned back against the counter's edge, trying not to look overinvested. When he finished, I told him what Alan had said. Pete's thoughts on the situation were, true to form, to the point.

"No," he said, slapping a slice of wheat atop his sandwich, the iceberg lettuce crunching under the pressure of his palm.

My mind was whirling, thinking of ways to clear the hurdles he was about to set before me, but I kept my facial expression neutral while he talked.

"I don't want to bring a baby into our family that's going to need a lot of special attention, taking time and resources away from Jack and Kate," he said. "I don't want their needs sidelined because we want a third child. It's not fair."

"I don't even know what the side effects of cocaine use are on a fetus," I said. "Let's at least talk to Dr. Chu before we close the door."

He said fine, not because he thought he'd learn anything that would change his mind, but because he knew I would do it anyway.

If you think these crumbs laid before me: *baby girl, cocaine use by birth mom, effects on fetus*, should've been ringing some bells, should've made me think of Debbie and her underdeveloped veins, the smallest the undertaker had ever seen, you'd be right. But they didn't. At least, they didn't affect me in a way that influenced my decision-making process. By the loosest tendrils, I made a connection between Eileen's baby girl and Debbie but dismissed it, thinking that Debbie had died in 1970, and medically, that was basically the Stone Age, and things would turn out differently for us. I didn't ruminate on what I knew to be true, a woolen yarn of truth so core to me it might as well have been woven through my vertebrae: Adopted baby girls whose birth moms used cocaine died.

Dialing Dr. Chu's number, I returned to pacing the back patio. I told her what we knew. Dr. Chu talked about the baby clinically, like she was just one of hundreds of thousands of drug babies born each year in the U.S., which, of course, she was.

"The baby could have deficits in some aspects of cognitive performance, information processing, and attention to tasks," she said, "But sometimes these kids grow up without any of these issues. I'm more concerned about the alcohol use, Denise. I know it seems more benign, but with heavy alcohol use, there will most certainly be delays."

Dr. Chu had gotten me through my first pregnancy, the birth of my first child, my miscarriage, and D&C. She was a trusted Sherpa. I hung up the phone and went to tell Pete I agreed with him. This wasn't our baby.

17

**LULLABY CLASS #1
LIFELONG ISSUES IN ADOPTION**

One Thursday evening late in August, we got a sitter and left for our first adoption class. I planned our leave-the-house time so that we'd arrive early even if we hit traffic. Lullaby was doing our home study, so formally or not, their evaluation of us started tonight. Having arrived in Orange fifteen minutes early, Pete wanted to grab Subway—he'd seen one just off the exit.

Fifteen minutes is a good amount of time for hanging out nervously in the car. Fifteen minutes is not a good amount of time to order Subway sandwiches. And then what? We would *eat the sandwiches?* Grapple with spinach leaves and swipe at mustard moons on the sides of our mouths in a room full of people we were trying to impress? "Everybody eats," Pete would say. When he pulled a u-ey, in my mind, I was screaming: *We are not getting a fu-cking Sub-way sand-wich!* But one of our Marital Issues was that Pete thought I was controlling, and my not allowing him to eat seemed like gifting him ammo. So, I told him to get me the veggie.

Lullaby's office was housed in a nondescript stucco business park. We walked through the door and into a small reception area where several couples were signing in on a clipboard and writing on name tags with Sharpies. After a couple of nervous exchanges, a woman entered the room and escorted us down a dimly-lit hallway that led to a bright, cheerful classroom. Four long, rectangular tables on each side of the room were separated by an aisle down the middle. Pete and I took our seats at a table in the back.

The woman who'd escorted us back introduced herself as Paula. Paula was in her fifties, tall and broad-shouldered. She wore a flowy patterned skirt and a long medallion-type necklace. Her dark brown hair fell in a shoulder-length wavy bob. Paula told the room that she was an adoptive mom herself, that she and her husband had adopted multiple children from multiple countries, Russia and Korea being two of them. She seemed to be making the case for how she and her husband had done it right. They often made foods—and had decorative items around their home—from their children's original cultures. Her adolescent daughter had once screamed, "You're not my real mom!" and Paula puffed up with pride when she told us she hadn't so much as batted an eye.

The woman sitting behind Paula, whom Paula hadn't acknowledged, was young, thirtyish. She wore a soft grey t-shirt, and her hair looped on top of her head. When it was her turn to talk, she didn't stand but introduced herself passively from her chair.

"Hi…I'm Emily. I'm brand-new to Lullaby, but I've been in social work for a few years now. I'm just learning the ropes, but if you're here for domestic adoption or doing your home study through Lullaby, I'll be your social worker."

Emily was a soft kind of girl, the kind of girl I knew I could dominate, but she was going to be our social worker, so the tables were turned. I smiled at Emily as she spoke, making exaggerated head nods.

Emily remained seated behind the table as Paula began the class in earnest.

"First, we will do introductions," Paula said. "Please tell us what program you're adopting through -- international, domestic, or snowflake; if you have children; and where you live."

I scanned the room, counting thirteen couples. I spotted the Orange County couple from Alan's Adoptive Families Gallery, Gary and Trina. 'Grow old with me; the best is yet to be!' was in the room! Seeing Gary and Trina outside my laptop screen felt like seeing a movie star in the wild. Another couple caught my eye. They were older, late fifties or maybe early sixties. I wondered if they were getting some kind of foster care certification. His hair was stark white, and he wore a faded, soft-looking denim button-up. Her hair, the color of steel wool, hung in a U to the top of her jeans. I admired how cozy her feet looked in woolly socks and sandals, my own feet bare and damp in flats. The man looked ahead. The woman looked down at her hands.

After introductions, Paula pulled up a graphic:

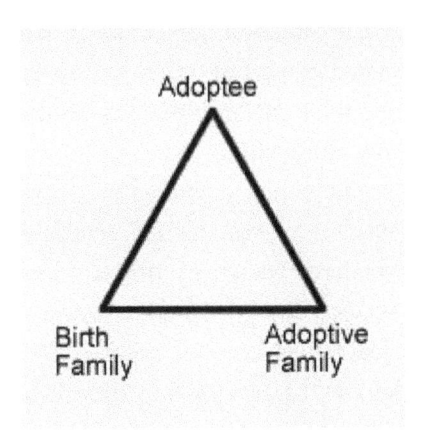

```
        Adoptee
          /\
         /  \
        /    \
       /      \
      /_____\
  Birth        Adoptive
  Family       Family
```

Below the triad was a definition:
"Members of the Adoption Triad are related forever – you are or will become an adoptive family which includes

yourselves, the children, and the birth family, no matter whether you have an open or closed adoption, or if you have adopted from another country or through foster care."

Looking at the definition of the adoption triad, I resisted it from both corners I occupied. As an adoptee, the definition felt false to me. My biological parents weren't family. They didn't even know me. I didn't know if my birth mom was alive or dead. My family was the people who'd loved me when I was bratty, self-centered, and withholding. The ones who'd driven three states to help me move into (and then out of) shitty apartments. My biological parents weren't family; if we passed one another on the street, we wouldn't even know it.

As a prospective adoptive mom, defining our birth mom as 'family' and 'related forever' was also uncomfortable. I wanted our baby's birth mom in our lives, but in a compartmentalized way, like sending her letters and photos. Other versions of openness I'd heard about—birth moms who came for Thanksgiving and Christmas or joined in on Mother's Day celebrations—I wanted no part of. I didn't want to share equal space in the triangle with our birth mom. I wanted to take up the most space in my child's life.

The fact that I wanted any openness at all wasn't for the benefit of the birth mom; it was for the benefit of our child. Growing up, I'd wondered what my birth mom looked like and what my story was. As a child, I would've asked her: Did you do it in the backseat? Was he your boyfriend? Were you a cheerleader and he was captain of the football team? As an adult, I would've asked: What was your pregnancy with me like; what can I expect? Do we have a history of breast cancer? I wanted our child to be able to get answers to their questions.

Paula moved on to the next slide, a diagram:

The Adoption Legacy

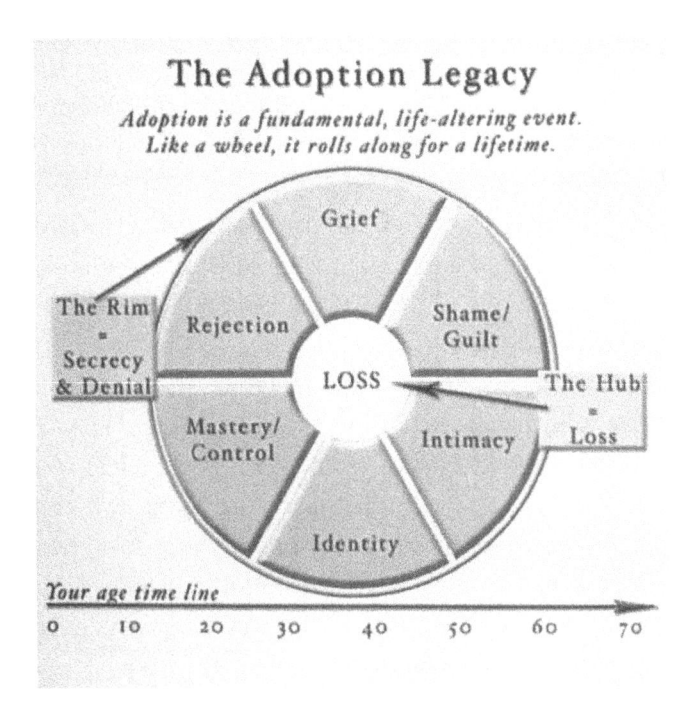

Adoption is a fundamental, life-altering event. Like a wheel, it rolls along for a lifetime.

[Diagram: A wheel divided into six segments — Grief, Shame/Guilt, Intimacy, Identity, Mastery/Control, Rejection — surrounding a central hub labeled LOSS. The Rim is labeled "Secrecy & Denial" and The Hub is labeled "Loss." Below the wheel is "Your age time line" marked 0, 10, 20, 30, 40, 50, 60, 70.]

(Sharon Kaplan Roszia and Deborah Silverstein, copyrighted 1986)

The placement of LOSS as the center of the adoption graphic shocked me. It was so *bleak*.

As hopeful adoptive parents, Pete and I hadn't experienced loss to the degree other couples in the room had, many experiencing years of infertility or multiple miscarriages, but the feelings I'd walked in with were positive: we were going to *get* a baby, we were *adding* to our family, I was going to *get to be* somebody's mama again. As an adoptee, I didn't relate to the LOSS wheel either. I didn't feel ashamed or guilty. I didn't feel rejected by my birth mom.

Looking at the wheel from a birth mom's perspective was the only vantage point from which LOSS seemed inevitable.

Counting us off by threes, Paula split us into small groups.

"Each group member is to share one or more specific examples of loss you've experienced thus far in your adoption journey," Paula said. "When time's up, you'll come back and report to the large group."

My group headed back through the hallway toward the reception area to complete the activity. Pete's group stayed inside the classroom. We exchanged *here we go* eyebrow raises as I headed out of the room.

I had Orange County Gary in my group. He spoke first.

"We were matched a few months ago with a girl in Arizona, but we decided not to pursue it," he said. "It just felt too risky." I was dying to know what had made them step away from a baby. His wife didn't look like a woman who would be scared off by much. He said they'd been waiting a long time; he sounded tired. I got the feeling a baby was her dream. I pictured the two little boys I knew Gary had at home.

The woman who spoke next, Lara, was twenty-six. Olive-skinned, with long, thick, bronze-colored hair in a ponytail, she was makeup-free and gorgeous. Her hot-pink tank top showed off her toned arms and pulled across her breasts. She was a ray of sunshine in the desiccated, fluorescent-lit lobby. I marveled that at just twenty-six she and her husband had already tried to get pregnant long enough to know it wasn't going to happen and agreed upon adoption.

"Our loss is that our family isn't happy we're adopting. Family members on both sides don't consider adopted children 'real' family," she said, air-quoting and gently rolling her eyes. She and her husband were moving forward anyway. I wanted to mother her (age-wise, I could've been her mother) and love her and her adopted baby like crazy. I hoped her a-hole family members would have a change of heart when the baby arrived or, at a minimum, keep their mouths shut.

When it was my turn, I worked in that not only were we adopting, but that I was adopted—to establish myself as an authority.

"We had a miscarriage last year that ended with a D&C," I said. "The hardest part was that we'd decided we were through. Done having kids. We were careful with birth control, but I got pregnant anyway. It just…it felt like another baby was meant to be."

On the drive home, I told Pete about Orange County Gary, that I'd been stalking him and his wife on Alan's website. I told him about 'Grow old with me, the best is yet to be!' but that he'd seemed sad and nice and I'd liked him after all.

Pete had the white-haired man in his group. He and his wife had adopted a baby boy, but after a while, the birth mom had changed her mind. A social worker came and took their son from his wife's arms. It was like a death, he'd said. It had taken her ten years to consider trying again, and he figured now they were too old for anyone to pick them.

We drove the rest of the way home, through the wide-open darkness, in silence.

18

Marcia, her husband CK, and their two-year-old son Dorian flew down to stay the weekend with us at the end of August. Saturday evening, we had mutual friends over for dinner, enjoying one of those rare nights in which the kids all got along and remained injury-free, allowing the adults to top off their wine glasses and relax. On Sunday morning, Marcia and I walked the lake to catch up on the things we wanted to talk about without the guys around. That night, as our weekend wound down, she was getting organized for their flight the next morning. I laid on the fold-out bed, propped up on my elbow as I watched her stock her diaper bag. We could hear the guys bantering back and forth in front of the TV and the thumps and footfall of Dorian, Jack, and Kate playing upstairs when Marcia walked over, softly shut the door to our guest room, and turned to face me.

"I've been trying *not* to tell you this all weekend because I don't want to get your hopes up, but I know someone who may want to give you their baby," she said, immediately bursting into tears.

"WHAT?!" I whisper-yelled because she'd done the shut-the-door thing.

Everything she'd been holding in shot out, rapid-fire: "I have a friend, a woman I work with, but she's in a different office. I shared your post on Facebook and she's been asking me questions about you guys. A lot of questions, actually. She wanted to know if you're really as great as you seem, and I told her yeah. She just went through a divorce; the ex is the dad, and he's already signed away his rights to the baby. They have two grown kids together, and she just doesn't want to do it all over again. She has her MBA; the baby's a Latino boy, and…she's due tomorrow."

"*WHAT??!!*" I screamed.

Tears were streaming down my face then, too, not only because there might be a baby, but because she'd kept her secret pent up inside all weekend long, even though the strain of it was *killing* her because she didn't want me to be disappointed if the story didn't end with me getting a baby.

Marcia's friend, Anita, had my phone number and last Marcia had talked to her—just a few days before—she still wasn't sure what she was going to do. But she'd asked for my number, so it definitely wasn't out of the realm of possibility that we could get a call from her the next day saying she wanted us to adopt her baby.

I wasn't even sure we were in a place where we *could* accept a baby. We were nowhere near completing our home study. I called Alan and regurgitated everything Marcia had said. He told me to call Lullaby to see if we could expedite our home study. Arizona, where Anita lived, required a completed home study, but even if we couldn't get it done within the next week or so, Alan assured us that there was an intermediary step in which the baby could stay in a foster home until it was complete.

It was 10:25 p.m. on Sunday night. Lullaby had given us an emergency number for situations like this. I got out the paperwork, found the number, and dialed.

"You have reached Lullaby Christian Adoption Agency…"

Fhuuuck!

I emailed our social worker, Emily, the subject line: *Urgent!* Mercifully, she called right away.

"We may be able to contract with an agency in Tucson to do the birthparent side of the work," Emily said. "But I can't get your home study expedited because of the out-of-state clearances." Because we'd lived outside of California in the past five years, Emily explained, Lullaby needed to submit criminal activity and child abuse clearance forms to law enforcement agencies in Iowa, and that hadn't been done yet.

"You can't take physical custody of the baby until you're cleared by Iowa," Emily said.

"What about the foster care step?" I asked.

"I've never heard of that," Emily said. "But I'll look into it and get back to you." I mentally cursed her newbie status as we said our goodbyes.

The out-of-state clearance snag threw me. I hadn't understood there were items on the home study 'To Do List' that were out of my control. But if our baby had to stay in foster care for a few days while we waited for Iowa to clear us, that'd be okay. We'd get a hotel room in Tucson and be with him every second they'd let us. It wasn't ideal, but it was doable.

It was after midnight when we finally went to bed, Pete and I upstairs, Marcia and CK in the room directly below us. I imagined a silk thread the color of Valentine's Day hearts running through the floorboards, connecting Marcia and me as we lay next to our husbands. I was giddy with the possibility that one of my oldest and dearest friends might have led me to my baby. I thought about how she'd been fielding questions from Anita for weeks and the loving answers I knew she'd given, allowing Pete and I to remain blissfully unaware of what we may or may not be given.

Anita kept her baby. I was disappointed but not surprised. I'd thought about her, tried to put myself in her position. If Jack and Kate were grown, and Pete and I were divorcing, and I got pregnant during separation sex, even if I couldn't stand the sight of him, it would be impossible to let someone else raise our baby, the brother or sister to the kids I already loved more than I loved myself.

The day we learned Anita was keeping her baby, I completed the forms Lullaby needed to request our out-of-state criminal and child abuse clearances. Lynda said it would be a few weeks before they heard back from Iowa. I was annoyed Lullaby hadn't informed us that the clearance was a deal breaker. Why hadn't they urged us to begin the process back in July when we first began working with them? But I admitted to myself that we probably weren't going to be contacted by a birth mom in the next few weeks, anyway.

Along with learning that Anita had been checking us out on Facebook came the happy realization that *Holy shit, our networking is working!* Women thinking about adoption were looking at our profile. We needed to be ready. And not just home study ready, but the *fun* kind of ready—gathering the items I'd wanted to turn my attention to but hadn't allowed myself: a bassinet, a car seat, formula, diapers, bright white onesies, and buttery sleepers.

At a second-hand shop I found a sweet, cream-colored bassinet with plush teddy bears hanging from the canopy. I brought it home and put it at the foot of our bed. We bought a car seat. Pete and I dragged the changing table out of the garage where it'd been housing baseball mitts and swim vests. He put a new coat of white paint on it, and we put it in my office/toy room.

I strolled the baby section in Target. I placed a container of Similac and a box of Pampers Newborn Snugglers in my cart like I had a baby at home. The shoppers around me *think* I have a newborn at home, I realized with a thrill. The Pampers were a splurge. With Jack and Kate, I'd always *wanted* to buy Pampers but ended up putting the store brand in my cart because I couldn't justify spending the extra five bucks when they were just going to shit and pee in them. But for our baby *out there*, I splurged. I wanted to smell and touch the baby powder-scented diapers while I waited for her.

As I checked out, I was filled with hopefulness. *I have a legitimate reason for buying these items. I'm not a fraud just because there's no imminent baby.*

A baby was on its way to us. I was sure of it.

19

Emily walked us through the room where she and Paula had led the adoption class before guiding us upstairs to her office to conduct our first home study interview. On the shelf behind her desk was a picture of her husband and her daughter. Her husband was Black. And *hot*. Maybe Emily wasn't the shrinking violet I'd pegged her as. Her daughter was J-Crew-ad adorable. A huge folk art print depicting a USC football game—white-sweatered figures waving cardinal and gold pom poms—surprised me. I thought of proud USC graduates as BMW drivers, not messy, top-bunned social workers. Emily sat behind her desk while Pete and I sat on the low, nubby couch pressed against the back wall. I was grateful for the distance.

I continued to scan the room for clues: Who was Emily? What was she going to ask us? Were we going to pass this test? On the floor to the left of her desk sat a car seat, the bucket type you only use for the first year. But her daughter was a toddler. It took me a few seconds before I realized, with a start, that the car seat was for the babies Emily took into custody. Whether the birth mom was half of a long-established match or a woman who'd only chosen parents for her baby from her hospital bed, it was Emily who picked up the babies. I wanted to touch the bucket. It was physical proof that it did happen: babies were born, and they were passed from their birth moms to their adoptive families, and sometimes, when that happened, a loaner car seat was needed. It was so practical. So *logistical*. I was jealous of every one of those pick-ups Emily had made and every one of those adoptive parents who'd lifted their baby from that pink and brown bucket into their arms.

My posture was not natural. I'd kicked off my flats and tucked my legs under my rear in a way that I hoped said, *We're casual*. I leaned my torso toward Pete in a way that I hoped said, *We have a very healthy marriage*.

"Tell me about your relationships with your families," Emily said. "Denise, why don't you start?"

I told her I was very close to my mom. "She's just a great mom. Growing up, she always made me feel loved more than anything in the world. She's one of those people who was born to be a mom—loving, nurturing. She'd do anything for her kids and grandkids."

"And your dad?" Emily asked.

When I considered my relationship with my dad, it felt loaded but also light—disappointingly flimsy. Selecting Father's Day cards had always been difficult; sentiments like "The Talks We Have" or "You've Always Been There for Me" didn't apply. My dad was a surface guy. The times I'd tried to get deeper with him had been met with deflection disguised as humor or sometimes defensiveness.

Dad left at the beginning of my freshman year of high school. After spending four years pissed off at him, I reached for him at the end of my senior year. We were given ten tickets for family and friends to attend graduation. I'd given Dad one, but he had asked for another for his girlfriend. Dad and I were parked in the carport of the duplex mom and I rented, his black Dodge Daytona—his post-divorce sports car—idling. I didn't want the woman he'd chosen over us at my graduation. But I did want the truth.

"I'll give you a ticket for Donna if you tell me the truth. Were you and Donna together before you and Mom got divorced?"

I already knew the answer. I'd always known in a way, growing up, because he was never home. He'd come home from work, have dinner, watch the news, and head back out the door. I'd stay awake until I heard the crunching of our Chrysler 300 pulling into the gravel driveway, usually in time for Carson, but long after we'd all gone to bed. But I didn't know *who* he preferred being with over Mom, Bob, and me.

The bookshelf in Dad's bachelor house, perched atop Tumwater Hill, held a photo album I'd never seen before. During one of my awkward visits, while I was in high school, Dad out front working on my diesel Rabbit, I opened the cream-colored album with gold trim. Inside were photos of Dad and Donna on a ferry. They were embracing—the wind whipping off the Puget Sound pushing their hair back from their smiling faces. Donna wore a plaid, belted cloth coat similar to one I'd had as a kid. The style was big in the '70s: dark brown on camel or navy on cornflower, with a faux fur collar. The date stamp on the back of the photo read 1979. I was seven. Dad wouldn't leave for another seven years.

"No," Dad said, his inflection falsely jocular, an angry amusement flickering in his eyes. "Donna and I met after your mom and I split up."

"Dad, *please*," I said. "I don't even *care* anymore; I just want the truth."

"We met after the divorce. That *is* the truth," he said, looking straight ahead at the back of the tool shed that doubled as the front of the carport.

I gave him the ticket, not knowing how to make a grown man tell the truth. I gave him the ticket ashamed of myself for not standing up to him, for not being stronger.

It wasn't just the cheating that made me lose respect for my dad. It was the '80s; divorce was everywhere—Stacey Crawford's mom had a live-in boyfriend named Roger; my favorite TV show, Kate & Allie, featured two newly-divorced-but-plucky moms, makin' it work in New York City. It was that he lied to me while I begged for the truth that left me with the shameful knowledge that my dad wasn't the kind of man dads were supposed to be.

"We're not as close," I said to Emily. "My dad's not a heart-to-heart guy. He was having an affair for most of my childhood and left when I was fourteen—they actually ended up getting married. As an adult, I see Dad and Donna as much better fits for each other than my parents were, but I was mad at him for a long time."

Talking about my relationship with Bob, I told Emily he was also adopted, that we talked about once a month, and that I knew he was there for me. (Which is basically true, except we talk maybe six times a year, and I'd like it to be more, but talking on the phone is so weird, and I hate it, and I think he does, too. But I *can* talk to him about anything.)

With my nuclear family out of the way, Emily turned to Pete and said, "Tell me about your family, Pete."

"I'm close to my mom," he began. "She lives in Chicago, so we don't see her as much as we'd like, but we're all close to her—Denise, the kids."

All true; I'd hit the jackpot with my mother-in-law. Carol was fiercely intelligent, curious, warm and welcoming, too.

Of his dad, Pete said, "He wasn't the greatest to us or to my mom. I wasn't speaking to him when he died."

By "not the greatest," Pete meant his dad beat his mom and made the kids watch. When ten-year-old Pete asked his dad to stop smoking at the breakfast table, his dad answered by flicking his ashes into Pete's oatmeal and making him eat it. The ash-flick oatmeal routine continued every morning for a week. The day Pete's dad tried to hit him was the day Pete moved out for good; he was fifteen years old.

Pete had four siblings: Mark, Luke, Paul, and Mary. He began with his sister.

"I'm the closest to Mary," he said. "She and her kids visit a lot, and we stay with them when we go back to Chicago."

Pete told Emily he was close to his next oldest brother, Luke, who also lived in Chicago. He wasn't as close to his two oldest brothers, Mark and Paul, he said—they were several years older than he was, had both moved to Texas, and weren't as easy to connect with as his Chicago family.

Everything Pete said of his siblings was true, but it was the first layer of the onion. He didn't mention that his older brother Luke was estranged from all of his siblings, except Pete, and I thought Luke was an egomaniacal asshole. Or that Paul was mentally ill, homeless, and traveled between Chicago, Wyoming, and Corpus Christi by bicycle or bus, depending on weather and cash flow, yet he was endearingly involved with our kids, sending them postcards, long letters, and even crumpled dollar bills from his travels.

Familial relationships covered, Emily looked down at her questionnaire and flipped pages, mumbling to herself, "Fertility struggles…coming to terms…that's not you guys…," until she landed on a topic she wanted to address. Emily folded the back page over the staple, pressed it neatly, and turned again to me.

"Denise, you were adopted. How were you told you were adopted, and what was that like for you?"

I gave the answer I'd given seemingly hundreds of times before. I always answered the question with pride in my parents because back in the seventies, they'd done it right. Even by 2013 standards, they'd done it right.

"There was never a moment I was told I was adopted," I said. "I just grew up always knowing that I was, and Bob was, and that we were so wanted and so loved."

I told Emily one of our family stories, one Mom loved to tell.

"When Mom and Dad went to pick me up, they met their social worker in a hotel room, and when Mom pulled back the blanket to look at me, I gave her a big grin as if to say, "There you are! Where'ya been?" As I told the story, the lines felt clunky, like marbles in my mouth. I'd never been the storyteller; I'd always been the adored receiver.

Then, words I hadn't planned to say came out of my mouth. I told Emily I did want to be different than my mom had been in one way.

"I want my son or daughter to not be afraid to ask about their birth parents," I said. "I want them to feel free to express curiosity about who their birth parents are—what their story is." I was crying, my voice shaking, "My mom said things like, 'Biology doesn't make a family,' and 'Blood doesn't mean a thing.' She made it clear that I'd be hurting her if I wondered about my biology or my blood. I knew if I showed an interest in my birth mom, it would break her heart, but I knew Mom's fear came from a place of love…she just loved me so much she couldn't bear the thought of sharing even one shred of me. And I get it. I love her for that…"

By then, I was sobbing. Emily frisbeed a pastel box of tissues to Pete, and he handed it to me. He squeezed my hand, and I kept going.

"But I want to be different. I want to be strong enough to tell my son or daughter, 'Ask me anything.' I don't want them to think that being curious will hurt me. And I know I will be because I know who *my* mom is *to me*...she's just my mom, and nothing could ever change that."

I don't remember anything else Emily asked us. There were a few more short exchanges, and then our first interview with our social worker was over. As we drove home, I replayed the unplanned confession I'd made in my mind. I thought I'd known everything we would say to Emily—the image we wanted to present, the information we would release. And then I was bawling about the elephant in my childhood: My mom hadn't given birth to me, and it wasn't appropriate or valid to wonder about the woman who had.

Pete wasn't surprised by my sobbing in Emily's office. I was blindsided.

20

August 28, 2013

Hello there,

I'm 25 years old and pregnant. At this time, I'm 18 weeks and four days. I already know the sex of the baby as well. I've been really thinking about all the different options I have, in order to make sure my baby is given the best life as well as the best of everything. I myself was adopted and it's such a beautiful thing to give to a family. At this time in my life, I feel that the best option would be adoption. I know it is a tough decision, so that's why I'm looking more into it. You both and your two children seem like a perfect family. Anyways, thank you again for what you all do and wanting to adopt. I live in New Mexico, and I'm in college full-time for animal science, then hoping to go to veterinarian school in Colorado. Feel free to email me back. I'd definitely like the chance to talk to you all and get to know you all better.

Lorraine

She was a college student! She was adopted! She was already halfway through her pregnancy!

Lorraine's voice was similar in tone to Liz's birth mom, Kat: a calm, young woman making a tough choice, but one she'd be confident in. I imagined Lorraine sitting on our couch, visiting when the baby was a few months old: she was happy to be there but anxious to get back to vet school in Colorado. She wore a new fuzzy-green fleece, and her still-damp hair smelled of Suave conditioner. Lorraine was no ham half-off.

I tried to figure out Lorraine's ethnicity by clues in her email. The two Lorraines I knew were both Latino. But her last name was Webster—that sounded super white. But she was in New Mexico, which had a large Latino population. Images of Lorraine and the baby growing in her belly began to rise in my mind like wisps of fog swirling in a crystal ball. I imagined Lorraine as Latino and her baby as a boy. People had asked me about the baby we would adopt, "If you could have any sex and any race, what would you pick?" And if I felt safe with the person— safe enough to tell the truth and risk sounding racist— I said I wanted a Mexican baby boy. I wanted to hold his chubby little body against me, caramel-colored and warm. I wanted to pluck my baby from a Diego Rivera painting.

With the emails between Liz and Kat fresh in my mind, I mimicked Liz's confident and light voice to answer Lorraine:

August 28, 2013

Hi Lorraine,

Pete and I are so happy that you contacted us. As you probably know from reading about us, I am adopted, too, so you and I share something very special in common. What year are you in college? Veterinarian school in Colorado is an admirable goal. We were just in the vet yesterday with Cooper (kennel cough)—they're amazing, how good they are with animals.

Are there any questions that I can answer for you as we begin to get to know each other? We'd love to talk to you on the phone if you'd like that. Just let us know!

Denise

p.s. I assure you we are far from perfect, but we are happy and loving! ;)

I sent the email on Wednesday evening. When I didn't hear back from Lorraine by Friday morning, I started to panic. I needed a hit—just a few lines from her to let me know she wasn't a girl who'd fired off an email to a couple she'd found online during a night of self-doubt, and then, with the light of day, realized that giving up her baby was, of course, crazy.

August 30, 2013

Hi Lorraine,

I was thinking…if you are just beginning to think about adoption as an option for you, feel free to talk to Pete and me about how the process might look and feel. You probably have a ton of questions about how an open adoption works, and we have learned a lot as we have been going through the process. For example, if you have fears about never seeing your baby again, that does not have to be the way it is (unless you want that). If you want visits, pictures, videos, and letters sent to you as you move on in school and your life, you can absolutely have that. Anyway, if you want to ask us questions, not even as prospective parents for your baby, but just as people who have learned a lot about modern adoption, we would love to talk to you.

Denise

She did not respond.

21

In Jennifer Gilmore's novel, *The Mothers,* the fictional couple, Jesse and Ramon, got an 800 number for birth moms to call.

"That's not really what we'll do, is it?" I'd said to Alan during our first meeting.

"That is *exactly* what you'll do," he replied. "We want birth moms to be able to reach you and Peter even if they can't afford a cell phone. Also, it's simply not wise to give your personal phone number to a birth mom before we have done a little vetting."

So, with a short application and a ninety-dollar sign-up fee, Pete and I became the owners of our own 1-800 number. When a birth mom called, it would route to my cell phone like a regular call.

I looked at our old 1-800 number phone bills recently and was puzzled to see a lot of incoming calls in July and August. We hadn't received a birth mom call in either of those months. The calls were made from 949, our area code, but I didn't recognize the number. And then I realized that I was the caller. I'd used Pete's office line, in our home, to call our 1-800 number every couple of days to make sure it was working.

But on a Friday evening in early September, a woman called our 1-800 number for real. "Hello?" I said, my heart slamming into my ribcage. *Where was 915???*

"Hi," a husky female voice said. "My name's Jennifer, and I'm pregnant. I found you on Craigslist."

I sprinted to the den where Pete was watching TV with the kids, stabbed at the phone and exaggeratedly mouthed: *"BIRTH-MOM."* I didn't have one of the birth mom questionnaires Alan had given us—I didn't even know where they were.

"Wow. I'm so glad you called us," I said, grabbing a legal pad and walking out the front door.

"I was in a long-term abusive relationship, but I got out of that," Jennifer said as I climbed into my Equinox in the driveway. I wanted to be alone with her, with no distractions. "I got a restraining order against him, but he ignored it, so now he's in jail. I was a bartender at Chili's before I got canned—I missed a buncha shifts because I didn't want to go into work with bruises all over my face."

I saw her pulling a Bud Light tap behind a Chili's bar, hiding behind Ray Bans à la Tom Cruise in *Risky Business*. I knew people who'd been fired for using their corporate cards to pay for vacations and furniture. I'd never known anyone who'd been fired because their face was purple from a man's fist, and they didn't want to be seen.

"Is the baby's dad the ex you have the restraining order against?" I asked.

"This baby's from a one-night-stand after I got out of that relationship," she said.

I'd exchanged emails with Eileen and Lorraine, but this was the first time I was *talking* to a birth mom. There wasn't time to be nervous or even to think—Jennifer's story was spraying out of her like buckshot: she was barely pregnant, maybe six weeks; after losing her job, her truck had been repossessed, and she was kicked out of her apartment so she was staying on an ex's couch. She lived just outside of El Paso. (My grandpa was born and raised in El Paso—was that a sign?) She was thirty-two and had two kids, ages three and thirteen.

"They're staying with their dad right now while I find a place to live," she said.

"I'm white," she said. I was grateful for her clunky disclosure. Did she know I wanted to picture this maybe-our-baby as we talked?

"I don't want any money from you guys. I was considering abortion…still am, but I was looking for options on Craigslist, and I saw you and your husband." She finally took a breath and said, "So, how does this work? Do you guys hop on a plane and come meet me?"

Jennifer sounded like she'd peed on the stick five minutes ago. If we flew to see her and asked Alan to begin the legal paperwork, that would be considered a match. The five-thousand-dollar match fee would be non-refundable, even if Jennifer simply changed her mind, even if she had a miscarriage. If we matched with Jennifer now, and then the Perfect Birth Mom called us saying she was due next week and had chosen us, we'd have to pay another five thousand to switch and be matched with her. You had to put your money on the right horse.

How would we know if a birth mom was a good match? If she was likely to keep her word? If she really wanted to place her baby for adoption or was an attention-seeker? Part of Alan's role was to help us match with the right woman at the right time for the best shot at success. He'd counseled it was best to match with a woman in her third trimester for three reasons:

1. Miscarriage is common in the first trimester.

2. When a woman isn't showing yet, the baby doesn't seem as real to her as when her belly is big, and she can feel it kicking, especially with first pregnancies.
3. Boyfriends and family can have a huge influence on a woman who's considering adoption. She can have every intention of placing her baby for adoption early on but get talked out of it.

But by the third trimester, Alan said, most issues have been worked through, and the timing is right for a woman to begin the legal steps required to place her baby for adoption. It was with all of the above swirling in my mind that I answered Jennifer:

"We would love to come and meet you! But you're so early in your pregnancy. Why don't we keep talking and emailing until you get a little further along and then we'll come and meet you, or you can even come to California if you want to get away for a while."

"I really want to get a plan in place; if I don't, I'll feel like I should just get an abortion so I don't get stuck with this baby," Jennifer said.

The differences in our vantage points came into focus for me. *If she only knew*, I thought.

Ever since Alan had told us eighty couples were vying for every newborn available for adoption, I saw us all as a crazed mob, straining against a locked and bulging nursery door, beet-faced and wild-eyed. When you're desperate for a baby, it's hard to imagine there are women out there who are equally as desperate *not* to have the baby they are pregnant with. But talking to Jennifer, I got it. She was a single mom with two kids. She was homeless, jobless, and without transportation. She may or may not have been knocked up by the ex who'd beaten her; the one-night stand thing sounded a little too convenient. The last thing she needed was a baby that needed her care when she couldn't take care of herself or the two kids she had. I heard the fear in her voice—she didn't want to end up with this baby by default.

"I *promise you*, you will not get stuck with this baby," I said. "Even if you don't pick us, there are so many people out there who are desperate to love and parent your baby. Let me talk to Pete and our lawyer, and I'll get back to you within twenty-four hours—does that sound good?" I needed to hit pause. My head was swimming.

She agreed, and we hung up.

I typed up an excited, detail-filled email to Alan: ex-boyfriend w/restraining order, Chili's, repoed truck, two kids. I was proud of all of the information I'd gotten without using his Birthmother Telephone Information Sheet, a three-page, single-spaced, scripted questionnaire Alan had supplied, saying it needed to be filled out to the best of our ability during the first conversation we had with any birth mom. But I found the idea of asking a birth mom during an initial call, "Do you do drugs? If so, what kind and how often?" off-putting. Plus, I figured Alan didn't often work with adoptive moms with my unique social savvy. I eagerly awaited Alan's response.

The first line of Alan's reply read: "Always helpful if you can get us the first *and last name* of the birth mom at the time of the first call so we can check our indices to make sure that she is not a scammer."

Right. Last name. Shit.

When I next spoke with Jennifer, Alan said to tell her that he'd send her some information about Pete and me and also a packet she needed to fill out and send back as a way for all of us to learn more about one another before agreeing to a match

(After I got her address, that is; I'd forgotten that, too.). After we had learned more about each other, *then* we would hop on a plane to meet her. He told me to reassure her that we felt her urgency but that we wanted to do everything the right way.

The next day, I sat with my favorite pen in hand and the Birthmother Telephone Information Sheet in front of me. Chastened, I was ready to follow Alan's instructions. I dialed Jennifer's number; she picked up right away.

"How are you feeling?" I asked.

"I'm waiting for someone to come out of the store," she said. "I can't talk long; they can't know I'm on the phone with you."

I heard the crunching of tires over gravel, the wind crackling over her mouthpiece. I imagined a wide-open gravel lot, Jennifer sitting on the hood of a muscle car. My heart ached for her—I knew what it felt like to be muzzled. Who was the person in the store? The ex who was giving her shelter but maybe expected sex in return? Restraining order ex? The father of her kids?

I told her I understood. "But I need to get some information from you. We'll just get through as much as we can, okay?" I asked her for her last name and added it to the top of page one, feeling accomplished. I was about to ask her question number two: "Estimated Due Date?" when she whispered, "Gotta go."

22

On a Saturday night in early September, we went to see Dave Matthews with our friends Scott and Amber. We'd met when we first moved back to California, and our kids were in preschool together. Amber was 5' 10", with long blonde hair, a classic native Californian. The VP of Operations for a large investment manager, she was intense and high-energy, but gentle and loving with her daughters and friends. Scott was laid-back, having been raised in Hawaii. Tall and good-looking, with dark, wavy surfer-dude hair, he was the only guy I knew who could pull off a Hawaiian shirt and not look like a dad on vacation.

When we first moved back to California, Jack and Kate didn't have any friends, so I threw a Valentine's Day party and invited twelve of their classmates. I got a few maybes; most people didn't RSVP at all. But I had ten hopeful little cellophane goodie bags lined up on our mantle, tied with white ribbons with red hearts. Amber and her daughter, Sara, were the only ones to show. After we frosted a few heart-shaped cookies, Amber and I abandoned the party schedule and took the kids to the park where they played for hours. The party was a success for Jack, Kate, and Sara; they didn't know it was supposed to be "more." It was a success for me, too—I've loved Amber with fierce loyalty ever since.

We met up in the parking lot to prefunc before the concert, and then the four of us climbed the long, winding path up to the top of Irvine Meadows, where we laid our blankets on the grass.

We bought crap beer from high-priced beer trucks, took blurry selfies, and danced to "Ants Marching," "What Would You Say," and every other song we had to move to. It was a good night.

On Sunday morning, Jack and Kate crawled into our bed at 5:45 to snuggle in a restless and elbowy way until Pete and I gave up and we all migrated downstairs to the coffee pot, newspaper, and the TV. I got a mug of coffee and watched ten minutes of Mickey Mouse Clubhouse before it occurred to me to check my phone.

September 8, 2013

Hi Denise,

I'm so sorry for the late response. I've been so busy with school, work, and my daughter. It's a little boy that I will be having, and he is due on January 26th. More than likely, I'd like to have a closed adoption…I guess that could change, but I just feel like this would be someone else's child and that they have the right to be the parents and only them. I know it was confusing for me as a child with the open adoption at first, and I know it was hard on my biological parents, so as of right now I'm definitely going with closed adoption.

Lorraine

Lorraine! It'd been nine days since we'd emailed—I wasn't sure I'd hear from her again. And she wanted a closed adoption. I'd envisioned our birth mom (and maybe birth dad) sitting on our couch many times. I'd imagined the awkward conversation we'd make as we watched our infant son reach for dangling toys, oblivious to the conflicting emotions of his parents, birth and adoptive, crackling in the air above him: fear and gratefulness, proprietorship and generosity. I'd understood that scene not only as possible but *inevitable*. A closed adoption meant we wouldn't have to navigate some of the difficult waters I knew were ahead. We wouldn't have to figure out what role our baby's birth parents would have in our lives. And if we had an open adoption and our birth mom had other children—as Lorraine just told us she did—who would those children be to our baby? When our birth mom came to visit with her children in tow, would we introduce them as the brother and sister of our baby? And how would that make Jack and Kate feel?

I didn't know if I had any biological brothers or sisters. I imagined that my teenage biological mom probably went on to have more children, a family. But if I ever met my biological siblings, I wouldn't call them my brother or sister—those titles had a shared history attached to them. Bob was my brother. He was the one I built forts with in the rec room, Mom's crocheted afghans serving as our rafts. He was the one who'd let me crawl into bed with him the night before we left for Disneyland when I was so excited that I actually felt scared. He remembered choosing ornaments off Grandma's tree on Mercer Island and summertime at Grandpa's, catching bullfish in the Nisqually and eating popsicles out of patchwork wooden bowls. Clicking through the View-Master of our childhoods, we saw the same images.

Having a closed adoption at the birth mom's request would leave Pete and me blameless; through no finagling on our part, we'd get to be our baby's everything. But what if he had questions like: "Where was I conceived?" "Do I look like anyone?" and "Why was I placed for adoption?" He wouldn't have anywhere to go for answers, and I knew that left a hole.

September 8, 2013

Hi Lorraine,

I am just so happy to hear from you! You have a daughter! How old is she, and what is she like? Are you close to your family, and would they support the adoption?

I want to comment on your thoughts on closed vs. open adoption. We 100% respect whatever you would want. You are adopted, so you have a greater understanding than many birth moms would of what adoption "feels" like. But Pete and I both want you to know that we are open to open, and even if you chose closed, and then you changed your mind and wanted to come and see him, or write him letters, or talk to him, we welcome that. Anyway, I just want to say again how happy I am to hear from you.

Denise

September 8, 2013

Hi Denise,

I do have a daughter, and she is 15 months old. She is just the smartest, greatest child I could have asked for.

I am very close with my family. My mom started crying; she was so thankful that I would even consider it. As of right now, the father is on again off again, but he is not ready to be a daddy, even though he says he is. He has lots of growing up to do! So, I'm trying to stay away from him and just trying to stay stress-free and healthy for this baby! The baby is kicking like crazy and hard. Sometimes it hurts a little. Other than that, the baby is healthy and growing fast.

Lorraine

I was thrilled to hear Lorraine's mom was happy she was considering adoption. I knew from Alan, the books, and every episode of "I'm Having Their Baby" that if a girl's mom didn't want her to give her baby up for adoption, it wasn't going to happen.

"It's almost impossible for a young woman to place her baby for adoption when her mom is telling her, 'I'll take care of the baby for you,'" Alan had told us.

I was pleased Lorraine's mom was, as I considered her to be, on my side.

Lorraine's description of the baby's father worried me. When she said she was "trying to stay away from him," I read that as she wasn't being *successful* at staying away from him but knew she should. Her description of him painted a picture of a young guy who was into partying, who wasn't ready for a family commitment, but still wanted Lorraine to keep the baby, not out of any real desire to raise his son, but in an ego-fueled performance of claiming his heir. I saw him as the enemy.

September 8, 2013

Hi Lorraine,

I love hearing you describe your daughter. You sound like an in-love Momma. What is her name? I am sorry that the baby's Dad is not the best support to you. It sounds like you still have feelings for him if it is still on and off, and I know how hard that can be, too. Do you think he would block the adoption if you decide that's the path you want to take?

Tomorrow is Jack's first day of kindergarten, so it's a BIG day around here. As we get to know each other, please feel free to ask us anything. We are happy to answer anything you'd want to know.

I hope you have a good week!
Hugs,

Denise

Lorraine had a nearly perfect profile. Alan had told us the ideal birth mom would fit several of these descriptions:

- Age 25-35
- Has given birth before: she won't be blindsided by the emotions of giving birth, the hormones, the connection she'll feel to the child in the hospital.
- Has children of her own: she'll know what it takes to raise a child—how financially, physically, and mentally draining it can be.

- Was adopted herself and has positive associations with adoption.
- Has placed other children for adoption.
- Has goals and dreams for herself: if a woman has a goal, she is less likely to think, "Why not raise this baby? I'm not doing anything else right now…"

Lorraine fit five out of six. Her being adopted was huge. Tracey—Dateline Tracey—told me their birth mom was adopted; she saw it as a very good sign. Lorraine was for real. She was almost perfect.

I Googled January 26, 2014, before I went to bed. If it all worked out, our son was due on a Sunday.

23

By mid-September, things were starting to click. Friends were sending emails, texts, and Facebook messages, reporting on how they were trying to help us find a baby:

Beth, a friend from Long Beach, had taken our flyer to her hairdresser, who'd immediately taped it to her station mirror. Beth texted me a picture of my family smiling back at me from a beauty salon in Sunset Beach.

Our friend Tracy, a colleague in Georgia, sent a message saying her hairdresser heard of babies all the time and had taken several copies of our flyer.

Meghan, one of Jack's daycare teachers in Dubuque, said her mom worked for a pro-life group and that she'd given her mom our information.

The captain of my drill team in high school, Jaime, was now a nurse in San Francisco. She'd sent our flyer digitally to every nurse and doctor she knew.

Another colleague, Allison, lived in Manhattan. She'd posted a personalized message with a link to our website on Facebook. Allison was a power networker—a woman who knew everyone and whom everyone adored. Having her engaged with our search was like having fifty regular people on the task.

Another woman we'd worked with, and another power-communicator, Nicole, lived in Ohio. She was seeing both her OB and hairdresser in the coming week and wanted more copies of our flyer if I could spare them.

It was exhilarating to think that even when we weren't advertising ourselves, others were doing it for us. The work of finding our baby was happening without us and across the country. I was deeply moved by the way close friends and even acquaintances were willing to go out of their way to help us with our search.

Emily was coming to the house on Friday the 13th to do her second and final interview with us. The purpose of the visit was to talk to us about our marriage and finances, to speak to Jack and Kate, and to tour the house. In preparation, I cleaned but not to an A-1 level—I figured if it was too clean, it'd seem like we were trying to hide something. We moved all cleaning supplies to the garage, and all medicines out of reach. We purchased a brand-new fire extinguisher and put it in the kitchen. We were ready.

Emily arrived mid-morning. After initial hellos and offering of coffee or water, the adults settled at the dining room table and Jack and Kate went upstairs to play. Emily placed a stapled questionnaire of several pages before each of us.

"You will fill these out independently, without talking and without making eye contact with each other," Emily instructed.

Pete and I nervously smiled at each other, caught off guard finding ourselves under the pressure of eyes-on-your-own-paper at our own dining room table.

What drugs have you used? What drugs has your partner used?

What do you and your spouse fight over? Money? Family? Personal habits? Does your spouse have an alcohol problem? Gambling?

Do you feel safe in your home?

After we completed the questionnaires, Emily talked to Jack and Kate privately. I wasn't nervous about her interviews with the kids. I knew I was a good mom. While I knew they might say something like, "I don't want a baby to live here," Emily was a mom and a trained social worker; she knew the difference between precocious and a problem.

One evening at the beginning of our search, Pete and I were in our front room; I was lying on the couch where I'd been reading, and Pete was sitting in one of our over-stuffed chairs. We were probably talking about weekend logistics or maybe something he'd seen on Vice when Jack came in and perched himself on the arm of the chair between us, resting his chin on the palms of his hands. He waited for a lull in our conversation and said, "Mommy, why do you want another baby so bad? Aren't we enough?"

Pete and I shot each other an, *Oh shit, did not see that coming*, look.

"That's a really good question, buddy," Pete said, throwing me a line, giving me a couple of seconds to think.

We hadn't told the kids about the miscarriage. Jack was four, and Kate was two at the time, and we felt they were too young, the concept too abstract. Or maybe we'd been lazy. Jack was a deep thinker; he would've asked good questions, like, "Was it a brother or a sister?" and "Why'd it die?" and we didn't have answers to those questions. But now my thoughtful and sensitive son was asking me, "Aren't we enough?" And why *wouldn't* he ask me that? I told them they were my world, my everything. My actions and my words didn't match, and my kids were very good at the matching game. "Why aren't you laughing for real?" they would ask me, and, "Why is your face smiling but your voice isn't?"

I considered for a moment that my five-year-old could possibly process the whole can't-find-a-heartbeat-D&C-passing-blood-clots-the-size-of-sea-cucumbers-subsequent-

depression truth, but I made a last-second zag to go age-appropriate. I leaned toward him.

"That *is* a good question, honey. You are enough. You and Katie are more than enough, I promise. But I just have this feeling that there's a baby out there for us to love. I just *feel* it. It might be a boy or it might be a girl. We don't know. But there's a baby out there that is meant to be part of our family. But if it doesn't happen, that's okay too, because you guys *are* enough, okay?"

"Can it be my twin? Because Bennett and Conner are twins, and I really want a twin like them," he said.

After Emily spoke with the kids, they went back to playing, and Emily, Pete and I settled into the front room to talk. The last time Emily interviewed Pete and me, I'd ended up a bawling mess talking about my own adoption. This time I was mentally steeled; I would keep the conversation focused on marital relations and retirement strategies.

But being asked about your sex life by a mostly-stranger is a trip.

"How's your intimate life together?" Emily asked with a cock of her head. "Satisfactory? Any issues there?"

"Satisfactory, yeah, good," I said.

"Very satisfactory," we improved upon in unison.

A more demonstrative answer would've been: "Pete makes me come every time. He comes too, unless he's faking it—do men do that? We do it pretty much the same way every time, and we're averaging about once a month. How's that bear out with other answers you're hearing?"

After the sex stuff, Emily wrapped up the interview and said goodbye to the kids. I walked her out the front door and down the sidewalk.

"Well, that's it for me," she said. "This completes your home study, except for your out-of-state clearance, which I expect any day. I'll get the report all typed up in the next few weeks. Congratulations!"

After saying goodbye to Emily, I paused at the pots flanking our front door to pull dead heads off the red geraniums, thinking I needed to put in yellow chrysanthemums for the fall. I pictured Emily typing up our glowing home study in her upstairs office with the nubby couch and the photo of her hot husband and adorable daughter.

We'd done it. Finals were over.

24

Four days after Lorraine emailed telling us that she wanted a closed adoption and she had a daughter, I wrote in my journal:

September 12, 2013

>Lorraine is 22 weeks now. I have not heard a response from her, but I think I will. She seems like such a great girl, good family, loves her daughter, adopted. We'll see...

But then, two days went by without any contact from her. My ideal level of communication with Lorraine would've been to hear from her every day, and her emails would've read: "I have picked you. You are going to be the parents of my baby. Don't worry; I have zero second thoughts. Have a great night!" But we hadn't even talked on the phone. We hadn't filled out the Birthmother Telephone Information Sheet. Email was where I felt safe, but I knew we needed to move beyond that for the possibility of matching with her to become real.

September 14, 2013

Hi Lorraine,

I just wanted to check in with you and see how you are doing. I thought about you often during the week, and I really do hope that you, Pete, and I can talk on the phone to get to know one another better. Would you like to do that?

Please let us know how you are doing--we think of you!

Denise

September 17, 2013

Hi Lorraine,

It seems that you no longer want to be in contact with us, and that is okay, but I will always wonder what happened if I don't ask you why. Did you decide against adoption? Did you choose another family to adopt your baby? It would be wonderful if you could please let me know where you are at (mentally) and what happened. Warmly,

Denise

September 17, 2013

Hi Denise,

I'm sorry I haven't been in contact. I've been so swamped with school and my daughter and my divorce. I have not decided against adoption by any means, just been very busy. I am talking to two other families as well. Again, sorry for the delay.

Lorraine

Divorce?! The Suave scent floated away from her hair. She was married. It was unclear if her daughter was the soon-to-be ex-husband's or another man's. Was she pregnant with her husband's baby?

And she was talking to other families. I'd been under the impression she was talking to us exclusively—that she'd been scrolling through Craigslist one night, half-heartedly looking for options, stumbled upon our ad, and felt reassured that adoption was the right choice because *we* were the right choice. Like when you fall in love with a gay man and fantasize that you can turn him straight? I thought that Pete and I, as adoptive parents, were *that hot.*

September 17, 2013

Hi Lorraine,

That is good news; we are excited to keep getting to know you. If you want to move to "the next level" with us, we should talk on the phone soon. Do you want to talk sometime this week or coming weekend?

You said that you are talking to two other families. That is coincidental because we are talking to two other pregnant women, too. But, I've gotta tell you--you are by far our favorite and most together. :) What do you like about us? What are you not sure about? Please ask us anything at all--we don't want you to have any unanswered questions or concerns about us.

Also, I am sorry to hear that you are going through a divorce. Is that from the baby's Dad?

I know you are crazy busy, but do me one quick favor? Send me your daughter's name and your address? The kids and I picked out some books that they loved when they were her age, and we want to send them to you. Warmly,

Denise

My *that's cool cuz we're seeing other people, too* response now makes me cringe, shudder with embarrassment at my immaturity and neediness. I justified it then by telling myself that we *had* been contacted by other birth moms: Eileen and Jennifer. Their contact hadn't turned into anything real, but still, I felt it was fair to say we were talking to other birth moms.

September 17, 2013

Hi Denise,

I'd love to set something up to talk to you all on the phone or Skype even. No, the baby's father is someone else. I've been going through this divorce for a while now, and it is stressful, but I know it's for the best. The father of the baby is still growing up himself. He's 25 but likes to drink too much, and so I keep him at a distance.

He says he wants to be a father, but he really doesn't act that way. I just want to make sure this baby has everything it could ever imagine. I know I could do it, but really, to tell you the honest truth, with all the stress from trying to make it work with the baby's dad, I feel more like I'm carrying someone else's child. I don't have a connection with this baby, and that's because I wasn't ready. Again, we can set up a time to talk. I'd love to Skype so it's like I'm meeting you in person.

Lorraine

We agreed to Skype on Friday afternoon. I was floating. Skype totally seemed like something that people who were successfully matched would do. Lorraine's email was satisfying in other ways, too. She sounded sincere in wanting to distance herself from the baby's father. And learning that her husband was not the baby's father was good news, legally.

Birth fathers occupied very little of my mind during our search. The birth mom was going to pick us—she held most of the power. Birth fathers didn't always have power. In California, there was a hierarchy to the legal rights of birth fathers. A biological father who was married to the mother had legal rights to the child; if he didn't sign the termination of parental rights, the adoption couldn't move forward. A boyfriend who paid medical and living expenses for the mother throughout the pregnancy had the same rights as a father who was married to the mother because he'd proven he was serious about caring for the mother and child. But a boyfriend who hadn't paid medical or living expenses throughout the pregnancy had the fewest legal rights. If he decided he didn't want to sign the termination of parental rights, or if he ignored the lawyer's attempts to reach him, the court could terminate his rights, and the adoption could be completed without his consent.

I was thrilled Lorraine's boyfriend was a drinker who said he wanted to be a dad but wasn't acting like it.

The next morning, the kids and I drove to the post office. I needed to mail another batch of ob-gyn and hairdresser flyers to friends. As I unbuckled Kate from her car seat, I heard the train whistle announcing an incoming email. It was from Lorraine. We already had the Skype date set up—this was frosting! Standing in the morning sunlight, I couldn't make out what she'd written. I stepped under the overhang to get a glare-free look.

"Here are a couple of pictures of him!" she'd written, attaching two sonogram images.

My heart sank. All of the nervous anticipation I felt toward our growing relationship with Lorraine drained out of me in one fell swoop and was replaced by nausea.

Though Jennifer Gilmore's novel *The Mothers* was semiautobiographical, I took that to mean that most of the scenarios in the book had actually happened since both the author and the main character, Jesse, had adopted a baby via independent adoption. And in *The Mothers* Jesse and Ramon were duped by several scammers who posed as birth moms. One of them insisted on sending Jesse sonogram images of the twins she was carrying, titling her email, "Yay! Twins!!!" The sonogram images the fake birth mom sent had no date, and the name of the mother had been cropped out. After Jesse and Ramon figured out that *Yay! Twins!!!* was a scammer, their agency told them that sonogram images—stolen from the internet, a friend, or a family member—were one of the weapons in a fake birth mom's arsenal. So, if a birth mom sent unsolicited sonogram pics it was basically a Huge Fucking Red Flag.

I studied the images with a combination of hope and horror. Lorraine's first and last names were there, but she had a daughter; she'd have sonogram images. All other information was cropped out, including the date. I'd intently studied the sonogram images of my own kids— wasn't this fetus a little too developed for twenty weeks? I didn't respond. I shoved my phone back into my purse, unbuckled Kate, helped Jack out of the car, and walked into the post office.

I never should've gotten this far with Lorraine without having completed the Birthmother Telephone Information Sheet, I reprimanded myself. One of the first questions was, "Can you provide proof of pregnancy?" But I felt like asking her that question would be insulting.

Or maybe I didn't want to hear the answer

Our Skype was scheduled for one o'clock. Pete's usual work-from-home uniform was cargo shorts and a ratty University of Dubuque hoodie, but on this day, he'd shaved, showered, and dressed in one of his date-night sweaters, a cashmere blend V-neck. He fiddled with his appearance in the mirror while I sat on the stabby wicker bench in front of our bathroom sink and blew out my hair. Normally, when we got ready like that, it felt flirty. *This is for you; I still care what you think.* But we weren't primping for each other; it was all for Lorraine. It was weird to be getting ready for—and desperately hoping to be liked by—a woman twenty years younger than we were, whom we didn't know. It felt awkward. And hopeful.

We'd exchanged usernames with Lorraine and agreed she would call us. We sat in front of our laptop at quarter to one and logged into Skype. We'd spent the thirty minutes prior walking around the house with our laptop, sitting in different locations to see which background seemed most inviting. We started on the couch in our den—that seemed cozy—but Lorraine wouldn't have seen anything but our crappy, metal, vertical blinds in the poorly lit background. *My god, was our den really that dark and depressing?*

We ended up at the kitchen table with the camera facing the front door. There was good natural light, and she'd get a glimpse of the wrought iron chandelier I'd gotten off of Craigslist and refurbished. I was pleased with how our faces looked on the screen. We were ready to meet Lorraine.

As we watched the minutes pass in the lower right-hand corner of the screen, my lower intestine gurgled with nervous diarrhea. I held it. The clock on the screen hit 1:00 p.m. Pete and I kept holding and then unholding hands. A few more minutes passed. I hadn't expected her to log on at 1:00 p.m. *on the dot*. At 1:12 p.m., I sent Lorraine an email:

Hi Lorraine,

We are here. Skype us when you are ready.

We sat looking at our own faces, smiling back at us.

Pete pushed back from the table at one thirty to go back to work. "Come get me if she calls."

I stayed on until two, when I had to go get the kids.

25

I was picking up the living room, shooting for two into the toy basket, when I got a call from a girl in Vegas.

"Hi, my name is Tara. I saw your guys' ad on Craigslist," she said. "I'm not pregnant, but I gave my baby up for adoption last year."

I figured she was pregnant but didn't want to tell me yet; she wanted to check me out a little.

I'd play along.

"I placed my baby with a family in Salt Lake City," she said. "They seemed really nice. They had other kids. They sent me pictures and stuff at the beginning, but now they're trying to break away from me."

As she told her story, I tried to fill in the blanks. She must be pregnant, I thought, and she's making sure she doesn't get burned again. She's feeling us out to see if we're the kind of people who'll take her baby and run.

"They're really strict, and I'm kind of second-guessing my choice, you know, of giving them my baby," she said.

Was she saying she wanted to take her baby back from the Salt Lake City family and give the baby to us? I knew that wasn't possible, but it seemed like that's where she was heading. I wasn't against it.

"My baby's about to turn one," she said.

In answering her, I tried to respond to the conversation that we were actually having, but also to the conversation I thought we *might* be having.

"I'm sorry this is happening to you. We wouldn't do that. We're open to having our birth mom in our lives. If she wants to visit, she can. If she wants letters and pictures, we'll send them. I love writing and taking pictures."

I was nailing this.

"I read your ad on Craigslist and you guys seem perfect," Tara said. "But how do you know you'll love your adopted baby as much as your biological kids?"

Holyshitwhat?

I took a quick inventory.

"I know we'll love the baby the same as we love our biological kids, really, because *I'm* adopted. I've never doubted my mom's love, even for a second. She devoted her whole life to my brother and me; she'd do anything for us. I just grew up knowing that, you know? So, it's not like there was ever even a tiny dark corner in me that wondered if I could've been loved more."

But I *had* wondered if Pete and I would love our adopted child as much, or in the same way, that we loved Jack and Kate. Pete and I would have a different dynamic with our adopted child than my parents did with Bob and me because we already had two biological kids. Mom and Dad didn't have any biological children—their love for us was the only parental love they'd known.

When Jack and Kate were placed on my chest, they were so tiny and helpless, still hot from being *inside my fucking body,* and I knew I would do whatever it took to keep them out of harm's way until the day I took my last breath, and I wanted to take my last breath preferably holding both of their hands. That all-consuming love just *was*. It just *is*. And I had wondered, will I love my adopted baby the same? Like, if I was in a Sophie's

Choice situation, would I push our adopted child into the arms of the Nazis? I didn't think so, but honest *honest*? I wasn't sure.

There wasn't much more to our conversation. I told Tara to hang in there and that she could call me back if she needed to talk. Just in case she was pregnant.

I called Alan. I told him that after talking to Tara, I seriously doubted our profile and appeal as a family. He was angry with her for shaking my confidence.

"It sounds like she is second-guessing her own placement," he said. "And she can't do anything to change that, so she called you and was looking for a little reassurance that the couple she chose will love her baby just as much as their biological kids. Or she wanted you to make you doubt yourself the way she is doubting herself. Forget about it."

His advice felt more fatherly than legal, and I was touched.

But I didn't forget about it. I imagined then that every birth mom looking at our profile was thinking the exact same thing: they won't love my baby as much as they love their biological kids. I'd hoped it would come off as obvious to a woman considering us as parents for her baby—that we'd love her baby as our own. But if I wasn't sure, how could she be?

After the call from Tara, my confidence was gone. We'd been searching for three months, and out of all of the contacts -- Eileen, Pete's friend Gina, Marcia's colleague, Jennifer from El Paso, and now Tara from Vegas -- Lorraine was the *only* one who'd led to anything beyond initial communication. After my conversation with Tara, Lorraine became even more attractive. She didn't question the love we'd have for her baby because she felt good about her own adoption. Our having biological kids wasn't a barrier for her. I regretted the defensive stance I'd taken with her after her Skype no-show. I'd sent her an email telling her we were wondering if her ghosting us meant that she felt scared, or awkward, or "Maybe this whole thing isn't real and you aren't really considering adoptive parents or aren't pregnant."

I decided to send another.

September 21, 2013
Hi Lorraine,

I wanted to tell you that whatever you are going through, we are here. If you just need some time, we will be here if and when you want to talk with us again.

I worked on our website today. I added some things that I thought were important to say. I'd love for you to check it out when you have time.

Warmly,

Denise and Pete

26

LULLABY CLASS #2
OPEN ADOPTION: UNDERSTANDING THE BIRTH PARENT DYNAMIC

As we entered the now-familiar classroom for the second Lullaby class, Emily sat at the front of the room, scrolling through a PowerPoint. Paula was nowhere in sight. I nudged Pete toward the front table—it'd bothered me the last time when we sat in the back. In my senior year of high school, Curtis Sumrock and I were voted Class Brown-Nosers. It never occurred to me to be embarrassed about that.

There were a couple of familiar faces from the last class, but mostly new. The couple sitting behind us was a couple I'd been stalking on Alan's website, Anne and Kevin. Anne was pale and thin, with dark, auburn hair cropped closely to the nape of her neck. Kevin was Asian, on the soft side, with a tight-shave haircut and a friendly face. During the first class, Pete and I'd stuck together during the break. This time, I was determined to compare notes with Anne and Kevin to see who was farther along in the process—to make sure we were winning.

Emily kicked off the class with a topic I was dying to hear about: What does the match moment look and feel like?

"Match moments are magical," Emily began.

Almost always, she said, she was blown away by the magic of the moment as birth moms and adoptive parents found amazing coincidences in their lives. She said in one match,

"The birth mom and the adoptive mom discovered they both loved Halloween!" In another, "Both the birth dad and the adoptive dad had owned motorcycles!"

I was torn as I listened to Emily reach for magic. I was so desperately curious about the match moment that I was hungry for every detail, especially the logistical: How did they get the call? Where did they meet? What did they talk about? How long did they talk before the match was made official? Who was with her? But I also wanted to believe in the possibility of the moment holding magic. But neither of the coincidences Emily gave seemed uncommon, let alone magical.

Emily asked for a show of hands of those who'd already been matched. *People in our class had already been matched?!* I thought we were all in the same heat of this race, just slogging through the home study. I hooked my arm over the back of my chair and turned to look at the room. *Anne and Kevin were raising their hands!* There was a couple in the back with their hands raised, too! All of a sudden, we were behind the curve. I'd been at home checking off items on my to-do list like a good student, but I was missing out on the real action. It was like sophomore year in high school when my best friend, Stephanie Key, and I were on the drill team with two juniors, Christine and Crystal. They were exotic to us because they'd had sex with their boyfriends. We watched them closely. Did they talk differently? Did they walk differently? What did they know? They'd done what we wanted to do but were too scared (we were scared of getting pregnant, popped cherry pain, and slutty reputations, in that order). Steph and I were dying to know how having "done it" would change us, and we were sure it would be fundamental, and at the cellular level.

As soon as Emily said, "Let's take ten," I turned to Anne and Kevin and said too loudly, "Hi! Are you guys with Alan, too? I think I've seen you on his website, maybe? We're Denise and Pete."

"Yeah—yes, we are," Kevin said. *Friendly.* "I'm Kevin; this is my wife, Anne."

I acted like I didn't already know that. Like I didn't know they had a chocolate lab named Oscar, and they took summer trips back to Indiana to see Anne's mom.

"Hi," I said. "So nice to meet you. Do you mind if I ask you a couple of questions about your match?"

"No, yeah—go right ahead," Anne said.

"*Thank you,*" I said in an exaggerated way that made me sound like Reese Witherspoon playing Elle Woods. "So, how long did you guys wait? And how long ago were you matched? What was it like—your match meeting?"

"We'd been with Alan for just over a year," Kevin said. "We got matched what…about three, four weeks ago?" he said, looking to Anne. I knew she knew exactly how many weeks ago they'd been matched, if not hours, but she only nodded in agreement and let her husband continue. "Alan called us one afternoon and said a girl had chosen us and that he was going to set up a time for us to meet."

Anne picked up the story. "We met her at a hotel restaurant," she said. "She was very young, sixteen. Her mom was with her. Mom was making all of the decisions—she was driving this thing, and her daughter was just kind of going along with it. It wasn't magical. It was awkward, and it was uncomfortable. Lots of awkward silences. But we liked her, and they liked us. She's having a baby girl. She's due around Thanksgiving."

I felt a white-hot stab of envy when Anne said her baby would be in her arms for the holidays, though her delivery of the information had been gentle and not at all boastful. I liked

Anne. I wanted to kiss her on the lips for her honesty: *It was awkward, and it was uncomfortable.* In those few words, she had released me from the expectation that our match moment had to be dreamily backlit and accompanied by James Taylor singing 'Sweet Baby James.' It could be real and weird and hard and guess what? We'd still get our baby.

When we reconvened, Emily was ready to talk about the reasons birth moms choose adoption. The bullets read:

- Untimely Pregnancy
- Awkward Pregnancy
- Unsupported Pregnancy

I could imagine examples of untimely pregnancies and unsupported pregnancies, but I was eager to hear what Lullaby considered an awkward pregnancy. Arriving at the bullet, Emily said that more adoptable babies than we might guess were products of affairs. A married man got his mistress pregnant, and the mistress placed the baby for adoption. Or a married woman had an affair, became pregnant, and placed the baby for adoption because she wanted to try to salvage her marriage. I'd never thought of affairs as a supply source for adoptable babies; from a consumer standpoint, I was glad to hear it. I considered what it would take for a marriage to get past an affair baby being placed for adoption, especially if it was the married woman who'd gotten pregnant (a married man could conveniently hide his affair pregnancy, a married woman could not).

Then Emily got to the big topic of the night: "Fears & Expectations Birth Parents Have of Adoptive Families." Emily explained that most birth moms wouldn't be confident enough to assert themselves into our lives after the baby was born, though most desperately wanted to be involved. She said it was our job as adoptive parents to reach out to our birth mom, to call her, to invite her to visit, and to do it over and over again if that's what it took to make her feel included in her (our?) baby's life.

There's a saying in adoption, "Before the birth mom gives you her baby, *she* has all the power; once you have the baby, *you* have all the power," and it's true. In California, there's a document called the Contact After Adoption Agreement. It outlines the level of contact and means of communication the birth mom and the adoptive parents have agreed upon. Are there going to be visits or letters and pictures? Will you communicate via phone calls, emails, or texts? It's not a legally binding document. It's a gentleman's agreement.

No, scratch that, it's a woman's agreement, because in every couple I know, it's the woman who organizes and executes human connection: birthday parties, dinner parties, beach days with friends, family Christmases, caretaking of elderly parents, all of these things—these hundreds of small and large acts of connection are usually taken on by women. So even though Pete was one hundred and ten percent on board with having an inclusive relationship with our birth mom (he was much more comfortable with it than I was), I doubted he'd ever have her number programmed in his phone. The Contact After Adoption Agreement was a promise from one woman to another. It promised, *I won't take your baby and run.* It promised, *Whatever agreement we come to, I'll honor it.*

Emily split us into small groups to talk about the fears we had regarding birth moms. Everyone in my group shared the same fear—that their birth mom would change her mind. No one mentioned they were afraid their birth mom would want to be in their life too much. Or that they were scared that having their birth mom in their lives would diminish their role as their baby's mom or dad. No one brought up any of those fears because the tone of Emily's presentation made it clear it wasn't okay to feel or say those things. This small group was a place to discuss appropriate fears, so I said I was scared our birth mom might change her mind, too.

On the drive home, Pete told me he'd had a single woman in his group who'd adopted a few years ago and was hoping to adopt her second child. Her first adoption story went like this: she'd talked to a birth mom who'd been about six months along, and it'd gone well, but the girl didn't end up choosing her. She went with a couple instead. The woman was disappointed, but they'd never been officially matched, so it wasn't a big deal. Three months later, she was outside washing her car when she got a call from a social worker saying the birth mom had changed her mind in the hospital, and she wanted the woman to have her baby after all. The social worker had said, "How fast can you be in San Diego?" The woman told the group, "I jumped in my car, ran into a Target, grabbed a car seat, and drove like a maniac to get my son."

That story. It was exactly what I wanted. Just, "Come pick up your baby." I wished I'd been in Pete's group to hear the woman tell her story firsthand—to watch the emotion dance across her face as she talked about getting The Call and the best Target run of her life. I wished I could've stood next to her so that some of her baby dust might've rubbed off on me. It didn't hit me until months later, when I thought back on the woman's story, that her dream come true had been another couple's nightmare.

As we drove home in the dark, I asked Pete what he'd been thinking when Emily said it was our job to reach out to our birth mom over and over again.

"I'm fine with her visiting a couple of times a year—and pictures and letters, that's just a given," he said. "But these classes are supposed to be helping us understand how the adoption process will go or could go, but really the whole thing's about how to make it best for the birth parents. I don't feel like they're designed to help us at all."

27

After completing our second Lullaby class, we were officially done with our home study. Emily had been to our house for the final interview and home inspection. Our fingerprints and physicals had come back clear. Our credit score and financial status had been verified. Book reports turned in. The only thing we were waiting on was the clearance from Iowa. Lynda—pink cardigan, taupe slacks—told us she'd sent our clearance request to the California Department of Social Services, which would process the request and then send it on to Iowa's Department of Social Services so they could clear us. The process usually took about three weeks, she said, so I circled three weeks out on the calendar and on the circled day sent Lynda an email asking for our clearance status. She responded:

September 26, 2013

Hi Denise,

I understand your concern about the timing. As a state office, the California Department of Social Services are not always available. Sadly, I was advised today that they are several weeks behind in processing requests due to staff shortage. Please know I am diligent and will let you know as soon as I have any information for you.

Lynda

P.S. Prayer is appreciated!

Everything about Lynda's email pissed me off. What did she mean, "as a state office, they are not always available?" I Googled the hours for the Department of Social Services in Sacramento; they were open weekdays from eight to five. Pretty damn available. And the use of 'sadly' has always rubbed me the wrong way. No one used 'sadly' sincerely. It's a mean-girl adverb. It's smug: "Sadly, there are no spots available," or "Sadly, we can't make it; we have other plans."

The situation we were in became clear. Our request was sitting on a desk in Sacramento—it hadn't even made it to Iowa yet, which meant we wouldn't be cleared for at least another month. If a birth mom, or Alan, called us and said, "Come pick up your baby!" we couldn't. I was livid. Were we going to have to pass on a baby because of fucking red tape? I knew it wasn't Lynda's fault; we were stuck in a bureaucratic logjam. But her frothy postscript of "Prayer is appreciated!" wasn't the battle cry I was looking for. I wanted elderly, perfumed Lynda to get on Sacramento's ass.

28

Our neighbor, Patty, knocked on the door. I loved Patty. I studied her as an example of the road not taken. She'd never married, never had kids. A retired court stenographer, she had owned her home outright for twenty years. In the summer, she golfed every day, and in winter, she skied every weekend. She organized her life, quite happily, around the needs of her Australian Shepherd, Moxie. Because of the no husband, no kids thing, Patty did what she wanted, and that afternoon, she wanted to talk. And not in the doorway; she wanted to come in and sit down. We settled on the couch in our front room, in front of the window that looked out onto the yard. Mom, visiting for her birthday, was sitting in the chair to Patty's left.

Patty squared her shoulders, slapped her hands on her tan, fit thighs, looked me in the eye, and said, "I might know of a baby for you."

"*What?*" I answered.

Patty wasn't someone I'd considered useful in our search. Nothing about her was maternal. I don't think I even gave her a flyer; that's how far removed from the world of babies and mothering she was to me. She must've heard we were hoping to adopt through neighborhood gossip.

"My friend Laura's pregnant," she said. "She just got out of an ugly divorce with an asshole of a guy, and she's pregnant."

"With asshole's baby?" I asked.

"No. With new boyfriend's," she said.

Patty was a conservative Christian, so the news of Laura being knocked up by new boyfriend was delivered with an eyebrow raise of judgment but was quickly followed by an exaggerated eye roll that said, Laura was her best friend, so *whatayagonnado*?

"She's forty-two years old, never had any kids. The jerky husband didn't want 'em," Patty said. "But Laura didn't really want kids either, and now here she is pregnant, and she's got no idea what she's gonna do. She mentioned adoption, and I immediately thought of you guys." Then Patty delivered the craziest part of her crazy news: "She lives in New Jersey, but she's coming out here to stay with me for a week. She'll be here in a couple of days."

We talked a little more—mainly Patty telling me she had no idea where Laura was in her decision-making process, and me reassuring Patty that I expected absolutely nothing to come of it whatsoever. But still. What an amazing story it might be. We'd tell it like this: At first, we didn't want to ask for anyone's help; we wanted to let Alan do the searching while we waited, dignified, by the phone. But then we said screw it and started begging friends across the country for help, and guess what? We found our baby through our neighbor *four doors down!*

Laura wasn't a young girl who'd change her mind on a whim. This was a woman with a stellar career. This was a woman who'd recently escaped an abusive marriage; she was just getting her freedom. A woman who'd never really wanted kids.

We made a plan. Patty would give Laura our DBML. I showed her where our website's URL was printed in case Laura wanted to check us out. We agreed we wouldn't plan a meeting because that would be awkward, to say the least, for Laura. She wasn't even sure she was going to place her baby for adoption, and there we'd be chatting her up and sneaking glances at her belly. I told Patty we'd be available all weekend if Laura wanted to meet us. I'd *make us* available.

I thanked Patty out loud for thinking of us. Silently, I thanked her for seeing us riding bikes, getting the mail, unloading groceries, and deciding that we were good parents. Good enough that she'd recommend us to parent her best friend's baby. I closed the door and wondered at how unpredictable, how lurching this ride was. An incoming call could be from a receptionist confirming a dentist appointment, or it could be from a woman thinking about giving me her baby. A knock on our front door could be a salesman asking if we'd given any thought to solar panels, or it could be a friend who knew of a baby. And even when it was a baby, as it had been with Eileen, Gina, Marcia's friend, Jennifer, Lorraine, and now Laura, it most likely wasn't going to end up being *our* baby. You just had to roll with it.

I sat back down on the couch, facing Mom. I knew she'd help me pull the promising pastel-colored ribbons from the story Patty had woven for us—that together, we'd hold them up and examine each one.

I looked at her with wide eyes, "What if, Mom?"

Without taking her eyes off her crocheting, she looped creamy ivory yarn over her needle, shook her head, and said, "You never know, Niecy; you just never know…"

29

One week after I sent Lorraine an email asking if it was possible that she wasn't really pregnant or considering adoption, she responded.

September 27, 2013

Nothing like that at all. I'm so sorry I am just responding as of now. My grandma is in the hospital. I've been with her every day. Then, to top it off, I was parked at a baseball field and was backed into by an older gentleman. I had my daughter in the car, but no one was hurt, thank gosh. I'm sorry again about our missed Skype sessions. I do want to do a session. When works for you and Pete? Again, I'm sorry for all the delays. This next time we will do the session, I am ready for it.

Lorraine

I had used sick/dead grandma to get out of stuff when I was in my early twenties. When I was living in Orlando, I wanted to fly home for a friend's wedding in Seattle. Katie and Kyle's wedding was going to be black-tie with a reception at the Columbia Center Towers. An Event.

But as a Thomson Holidays rep schmoozing British families into springing for the 4-Day Park Hopper, I didn't get vacation days. So I called my boss, Jim—a Scot and a really decent guy— and told him my grandma had died, and so, *sadly*, I needed to be on a Friday morning flight home. Grandma had died from ovarian cancer the previous year, and I knew she'd be okay with me using her this way. Grandma adored her grandkids, and she adored formality—she would've wanted me to go to a black-tie reception at the Columbia Center.

September 27, 2013

Lorraine,

We are so glad to hear from you and to know that none of the things that we feared kept you away. I am sorry to hear about your Grandma. I know it can't be easy to see someone you love in the hospital. I lost my favorite Grandma when I was your age. She was amazing-- Grandmas are precious.

We'd love to set up a time to Skype. I will call you tomorrow. Again, we are so glad to hear from you. I am glad that you are okay after all of the stuff (crap??) you have been through this past week. And I am glad that you have chosen to keep us in your life.

Denise & Pete

September 28, 2013

Hi Denise,

You can call me anytime you'd like. I am 22 weeks and five days as of today, and this pregnancy is real. I think that would be just a horrible thing to do to a family—pretend that you are pregnant; I could never do that. I do want to Skype, but you can call me as well. I can send you all pictures. I have a video of him moving in my belly that I'd love to send to you all if it allows me to.

Lorraine

We set up a time to talk the next day. I was determined to complete the Birthmother Telephone Information Sheet. I felt like I was dating Lorraine behind Alan's back.

"Hello?" Lorraine answered.

Both of us were nervous, laughing heartily at things that weren't funny: kids, school, being *so busy*. With Alan's questions in front of me, I fired away. She answered the invasive questions easily and openly. She was Hispanic, 5' 2". She'd had a couple of cigarettes before she knew she was pregnant, but no alcohol. The baby's dad, Jared, was Hispanic, 5' 10", and had been a baseball player. He was going to community college. Lorraine lived in an apartment with her daughter, Gemma, her older sister, and her sister's two young daughters. I imagined a cramped feminine space—a living room strewn with pink plastic toys, a My Little Pony nightgown poking through a waffled laundry basket.

Lorraine was adopted at eighteen. Her biological mom was into drugs. "She was never really there for me—to take care of me," Lorraine said. "She tried off and on for years, then finally, our family friends decided they were going to adopt me." Her adoptive dad was a doctor, and her adoptive mom was a nurse. She still had contact with her biological mom, but she was, "still kind of messed up," Lorraine said.

I absorbed the things Lorraine told me through a self-serving filter. I was happy to hear her dad was a doctor and her mom was a nurse—highly educated people were more likely to encourage their daughters to place their babies for adoption. But I was disappointed to learn Lorraine had been adopted as an adult; I thought she'd been adopted as a baby. I felt like she wasn't really *adopted* adopted.

After forty-five minutes, we laughed that we'd talked so long and agreed on a Skype time the next day.

Pete and I didn't get as ready this time. I did make-up, but no blow-out. Pete shaved, but no date night sweater. Lorraine logged into Skype at 1 p.m. on the dot.

She looked how she sounded: both cute and pretty, with a cheerful, eager-to-please smile, big brown eyes, and dark brown hair that hung to her waist. Using the camera on her laptop, she walked around the apartment, giving us a tour. It was endearing the way she was so open with her home. She showed us the kitchen with a drying rack full of neatly stacked dishes, then, turning around, showed us the room where they watched TV on a single cream-colored couch.

She slowly panned the wall where she and her sister had taped up their daughters' artwork— drawings of dogs, giraffes, and rainbows. A picture of a stick-figure family holding hands caught my eye. Names were written under the stick figures: the woman was Lorraine, the little girl was Gemma, and the man was Jared.

My heart dropped. I'm sure flashes of distaste and confusion crossed my face before I remembered that Lorraine could see me. She had never alluded to the baby's father—Jared—as anything more than a guy who drank too much and wasn't ready to be a father. Someone she knew she should stay away from. But stick figure Jared was a totally different Jared. This guy was standing under a rainbow and sunshine. He was smiling. Lorraine was smiling. Gemma was smiling. They were a *family*.

When I focused back in, Lorraine was saying, "Do you want to see him?" and pulling her beige cotton shirt over her bump. It was a pregnant belly, round and firm. But the anxiety I felt over the sonogram pictures didn't disappear; it just morphed into anxiety over whether the story we had on the baby's dad was accurate. One of the questions I'd asked Lorraine was, "Will the father give his consent?" She'd answered, "I don't know," but I'd skated over that. It didn't give me pause because if he wasn't living with Lorraine or providing financial support, he couldn't block the adoption. I was pulling for Jared to be a loser.

But if Lorraine was in love with him? If Jared was an attentive boyfriend and was filling the role of daddy for Gemma, and by the looks of the drawing, he was, Lorraine might not have had any real intention of placing her baby for adoption. Even if a part of her felt like it was the right thing to do, her emails to us may have been just "trying on" adoption.

I tried on engagement when I was twenty-two, with Joey, the DJ from the cruise ship. I'd only dated Washington guys up to that point—earnest Timberland-wearing boys whose parents were still together and lived in places like Mukilteo or Federal

Way. Joey wore a crushed-velvet chain wallet and bleached his roman-styled hair platinum (think Eminem). He grew up in a Florida trailer park with his older brother, Eric, and their long-suffering mom, Kathy. He told me about the rave scene where he and his friends took ecstasy and danced and shoved Vicks Vapo sticks in their noses and walked out of the club and into the sunlight at 6 a.m. When his contract was up, he asked me to move back to Orlando with him.

"Being on the ship sucks," he said. "It's such a stupid, fake life."

"Yeah, it *sucks*," I parroted back to him, even though I loved my job and almost everything about living on the ship.

We arrived in Orlando that fall. The following spring, Joey picked me up from my job at Calvin Klein in the Bealls Outlet mall to take me to lunch. I *really* wanted to go to Taco Bell like we usually did, but he wanted to go someplace nice, so we went to Pizza Hut. I was huffy about not getting my bean and cheese burrito, but in between breadsticks and personal pan, Joey pulled out a ring box and asked me to marry him. We'd picked the ring out a few months before at a pawn shop in Clearwater—a diamond chip with a black speck in the center. I said yes, we ate our pizzas, and he dropped me back off for the rest of my Eternity-scented shift.

I loved Joey and was loved by him, but it was an obsessed, jealous kind of love, not an I-can-see-you-being-a-really-good-dad-I-want-to-marry-you kind of love. I never called my parents or told girlfriends back home I was engaged, because it wasn't real. Joey never called me out on that, because he knew it wasn't real. We were playing engaged. We broke up, and I was back on the ship the following year.

After the Skype session with Lorraine, which, to an outside observer, would've looked like it'd gone fabulously—lots of laughter and never a lull in the conversation—happiness wasn't my overriding emotion. It was dread.

That night I sent Lorraine an email telling her how much we'd loved talking to her, "We are so excited at the thought of parenting your baby boy. It would be a dream come true for us. You would bring us joy that we could never come close thanking you enough for."

And then, because she'd told us she raised wolves on her soon-to-be ex-mother-in-law's property, I added, "Over dinner tonight, Pete and I were talking about how cool it is that you have wolves. I like people who are different, who like and do things that other people don't do, and having wolves is definitely different!"

The wolf bit takes me back to my seventh-grade year when I had a tight perm, big feet in white rain boots, and braces, and I would've said anything to be included in the Forenza circle. (But goddammit, Karrie Pidone, we had fun drinking grape Kool-Aid from your old baby bottles and watching *Let's Make a Deal*, didn't we?)

Pete and I woke up the next day to an email from Lorraine. She'd chosen us.

September 30, 2013

Denise,

I just know that you guys are truly the best and I don't need to talk to anyone else in order to find my son a great loving family. Thank you for telling me you'd give me time to think about all of this, but I do know you guys will be perfect.

Lorraine

Pete smiled, and I screamed.

The stick figure family on the wall was just a child's drawing. We were real. Lorraine's decision to focus on raising the daughter she already had was real. Our son was in New Mexico. Just ten hours east.

Pete gave me one last hug before going up to his office for the day.

The moment felt smaller than I'd hoped. Probably because I'd played out the scene in which we got The Call a million times, never once imagining we'd get An Email.

But who cares?!

Lorraine chose us.

That night, I went to Target for a few things to put in a care package for Lorraine, Gemma, and our baby. I Googled the weather in Las Cruces; it got cold at night. I wanted to find warm pajamas for Lorraine with wolves on them, but foxes were the thing that fall, so I chose aqua-colored PJs with black foxes on them, hoping Lorraine might interpret them as wolves. I imagined the top pulling snugly across Lorraine's belly, keeping our baby warm. I wanted to get something for Gemma, too, a little stuffed wolf and some candy. I went to the Sweet Factory in the mall, where they had bins of sweets and several stuffed dogs to choose from. I lined them up and stood comparing them for twenty minutes, contemplating which dog looked most like a wolf. I was the only person in the shop, and for a while, the sales girl stayed alert to questions I might have, but after several minutes, she gave up on me, slumped onto her stool, and started texting. I settled on a German shepherd.

30

A few days later, our friends Emilie, Mikael, and their two boys visited from Dubuque. Emilie and I'd become friends at the office. She was a tall blonde with broad shoulders–quintessentially Swedish. She had a fantastic, throaty laugh and a Ph.D. in Mathematics. One summer afternoon, sitting in front of our house, watching the kids play with sidewalk chalk, we were talking about our ideal places to live. Emilie said she'd live in Minnesota, where she'd grown up, and could hunt for their meat. In the same conversation, she told me she and Mikael's favorite date was to go out on a snowy night, wearing headlamps, and mountain biking through the trees. I remember thinking I'd never met anyone like her and wanting to hang on to her.

As the kids got reacquainted upstairs, we told Emilie and Mikael about Lorraine. Emilie enthusiastically told us that another couple they were friends with was also due on the 26th.

That bummed me out. Emilie was a thoughtful friend—she'd check in with me on the 26th, and if things hadn't worked out, I wouldn't want to think about her other friends holding their baby.

The next morning, we went to Salt Creek beach. We laid out blankets and towels, and Emilie and I lathered the kids up with sunscreen before they ran off to collect rubbery ropes of seaweed with their dads. We were leaning back on our elbows, taking it all in, when she said, "I think I'll go in."

I need to tell you something about Southern Californian women of a certain age: We go to the beach, but we don't go in the water. We hang out. We wear sun hats and cover-ups. We bring umbrellas, beach toys, sunscreen, Bluetooth speakers, and potluck meals with plates, cutlery, and napkins. We watch as our kids, and sometimes husbands, jump in the water, but we don't. For me, it's an *I hate being cold* thing, but more than that, it's a body image thing. I wish I was more toned. Or a few pounds lighter in my belly or in the bumpy fold below my ass. So I hide under my cover-up, and it's not weird because all the other moms are hiding, too. But Emilie wasn't a Southern Californian mom; she'd brought her family from Iowa, and she was going in. I followed.

October was the tail end of our summer, and the water was warm. We walked out until the sand slipped away beneath our toes, and then Emilie dove headfirst into the waves to body surf. I followed her again. Every other attempt, we came up laughing, not having caught the wave at all, but having been pummeled to the ocean floor. We scooped fistfuls of sand out of our cleavage and our crotches. We played in the ocean like I hadn't in decades. When we got tired, we floated on our backs and then treaded water and talked as the sun warmed our shoulders and waves lapped against our chests. After a while, Emilie swam back to shore, but I stayed out. I felt buoyant–physically and in spirit. From beyond the surf, I saw Pete, Kate monkey-gripped on his back, as he dug a moat with Jack. I waved, and they waved back. I saw Emilie, Mikael, and their boys laughing at a seagull tugging at our bag of salt and vinegar chips. I floated, weightless, letting the pregnant swells carry me toward the shore and the current pull me out again, in control of nothing.

The next morning, we went to the Aquarium of the Pacific in Long Beach. We drove separately from Emilie and Mikael so that we could leave early to be home for our afternoon Skype with Lorraine. She was going to introduce us to Gemma, and she and Gemma were going to meet Jack and Kate. We watched a scuba diver feed sharks and eels in the two-story tank and touched stingrays as they glided under our fingertips. The kids ate pirate-themed boxed lunches. After the jellyfish section, we said our goodbyes and made the forty-five-minute drive back down the I-5.

We settled at the dining room table. Pete and I side by side, Kate on Pete's lap and Jack on mine. We practiced.

"Say, 'Hi, Lorraine!' Pete said, waving Kate's chubby, three-year-old hand with his. Say, 'Hi, Gemma!" I singsonged, squeezing Jack and waving at the blank screen.

We kept the kids on our laps until five after and then let them go play.

I was pissed. Pissed that we'd left our friends early. Pissed that we'd fought traffic to get home. Pissed at myself because I'd been short with my kids, getting them spit-shined to meet Lorraine and her daughter. And she hadn't even texted to say, "Hey, sorry, I can't make it." I was spurned-lover angry. I was embarrassed she hadn't shown.

Pete wasn't bothered.

"It's probably weird for her to Skype with us—she probably just got nervous," he said, taking the steaks out of the fridge. "She's either gonna give us her baby, or she's not. We don't have control over that."

Ooooh, okay, Mr. Super Chill—is that how this goes?

I wanted to pat his naïve little head. He was blissfully unaware of the *finessing* it had taken me to get us this far with Lorraine. Pete had been given the Cliff Notes of the phone calls, the texts, and the thirty-nine emails she and I had exchanged. That was the level of detail he wanted, but also all that I wanted to give. I didn't want his opinion on Lorraine's slippery viability. We could get to the finish line if I just kept *handling* her correctly. We needed to show her that we cared about both her and her baby. That we had a deep desire to parent her baby. That adoption was the right choice, even in her moments of doubt. That we were cool for our age. And all of this information, this *data*, needed to be parceled out in just the right increments to make her *give us her baby.*

"Let her go, hon," Pete said, peeling the husks off the corn and tossing them into the trash.

I nodded my head and said, "Yeah, you're right," while violently disagreeing with him, crafting my next email, and thinking about what kind of cute care package I could put together.

I waited forty-eight hours before I sent this:

October 8, 2013

Hi Lorraine,

I wanted to check in with you and see how you are. We were disappointed you were not there to Skype on Sunday, but we are not mad. It just got us feeling like we want to know what is really going on with you. Are you freaked out by the possible adoption and you need some space? Is the baby's dad in your life, and maybe you are confused right now?

Is there anything we can do to help you? Pete said it must be a little weird to talk to us via Skype, and I agree.

It is a little weird for us, too. :) I just want to leave you saying that I am sure there are things in your life that pull you down or are draining, and we don't want to be one of those things. We want to help you if we can, and we want you to trust us and tell us what's up. We don't expect you to be perfect; we want to know you for real.

Hugs,

Denise

When I wrote, "I am sure there are things in your life that pull you down or are draining," I was trying to bash Jared. I was sure that without him in the picture, Lorraine would be certain of her decision to place her baby for adoption.

She didn't respond.

I felt then that Lorraine was the kind of girl who would string us along and then change her mind in the hospital. I didn't want to go through that. I decided I wouldn't reach out to her again. I would move forward as if she'd never said she's chosen us.

10/10/2013 DBML sent to Angela

31

Inspired by Randall Hicks' book, I sat down at our dining room table and Googled, 'women's shelters in Orange County.' Hicks said shelters could be a good place to drop off flyers and business cards. I was going to kick it up a notch. Since I was adopted and hoping to become an adoptive mom, I was going to offer myself as an adoption speaker.

The first two directors I spoke with were encouraging. Both agreed to post our flyer in their common areas and said they'd be happy to tell their on-site counselors about us. The third director I spoke with, Lauren, at Grandma's House of Hope, was even more enthusiastic about helping us connect with a possible birth mom.

"We specialize in helping women get out of sex trafficking and often accept pregnant women," Lauren said. "Send me several of your flyers."

I considered the term, 'sex trafficking.' What did it mean, *exactly*? The term conjured up a TV image, à la 60 Minutes, of Southeast Asian women crammed into the trunk of a car, lights sweeping over scared eyes. After a little research, I understood sex trafficking was another way of saying forced prostitution and that the vast majority of sex trafficking's victims were women and children. Shared Hope International, a nonprofit organization that worked to prevent sex trafficking, defined it as "When someone uses force, fraud or coercion to cause a commercial sex act with an adult or causes a minor to commit a commercial sex act."

Would I be okay with adopting a baby that was the product of prostitution? I thought about the act itself—some skeevy guy paying to come. A woman or girl trapped underneath him, physically and financially forced to take what he released. And a baby was made. Could I love that baby? The answer was yes. I wanted to love every baby that'd ever come from sex trafficking and needed a home.

The power of nurture over nature, or at least the balance between nurture and nature, was a theme that came up often as we searched for our baby who would have someone else's DNA. As I considered adopting a baby that was the product of prostitution, I thought about the biological parents. The father's character was shit. He saw women as objects to be purchased and consumed for his pleasure. He was controlling and possibly violent. And what about the baby's mom? I was more compassionate when considering the mother—forced prostitution wasn't a choice. But still, I wondered—how did she get there? Was she dimwitted? Weak? The parentage wasn't ideal. But what did *that* mean? Did it mean the baby would turn out to be a misogynistic, violent asshole? Or a little girl with low self-esteem and a proclivity for bad decision-making sewn into her DNA? I didn't think so.

I'd read a study in which scientists had reviewed nearly every identical twin study done in the previous fifty years, and, as a whole, they showed that about fifty percent of an individual's character and personality traits were genetic, and the other half were environmental. In other words, when it came to nature versus nurture, it was a draw. And I was banking on the fact that my nurturing skills were strong—when it came to molding my child's character and personality, I figured I could ratchet the nurture percentage points up to sixty-five percent, at least.

But what would Pete say?

Around noon, he came out of his office to make lunch. I was sitting at the dining room table with my massive adoption binder splayed in front of me, a yellow legal pad scribbled with shelter notes to my left. He pulled a plate from the cupboard, clanking it on the tile countertop.

Trying to sound casual, I said, "Would you be okay with adopting a baby that was, uh…the result of sex trafficking?" (I specifically didn't use the word prostitution, hoping he'd have a somewhat murky understanding of sex trafficking's meaning like I did.)

"Sure. It's not the baby's fault," he said.

On my last call of the day, I spoke with a woman named Audrey, the program coordinator at Precious Life, a homeless shelter for pregnant girls.

"Most of our girls have already given birth and are keeping their babies," she said. "But I'd love to have you come in and speak to the girls—to expose them to someone who's had a positive adoption experience."

I'd offered myself as a public speaker as a Trojan Horse—a way to meet pregnant girls and show them the picture of the four of us in the front yard with Cooper. But Audrey had called my bluff, and I wanted to do a good job. I had one month to prepare.

> 10/15/2013 DBML sent to Jodie

32

November 1, 2013

Hi Lorraine,

I just wanted to check in and say hi. I was thinking about how you are in your third trimester now and I just wanted to send you an email and say hello. How are you?

We are not mad at you, and we have absolutely no expectations of adopting your baby, so don't feel weird about emailing back. This is truly just a hello, and we hope you are doing well.

Denise & Pete

November 1, 2013

Hi Denise,

I'm sorry. I've been up and down a lot lately. I'm not with the birth father, nor do I intend on ever being with him again. My soon to be ex-husband's mom died on the ninth, and I was really close to her, so I've been very upset lately. The baby's father is making things very difficult for me by texting me mean things and being just crazy. I had to move back in with my parents due to that craziness, and now I'm just trying to be happy again. I'm sorry again for not writing back or getting on Skype. I tried to pick up your letters you sent, but the post office said they returned them to you on the 10th. I've just been so busy and trying to get everything done.

Lorraine

November 2, 2013

Lorraine,

We are glad to know that you are okay. Being at your parents is the best place for you to be, even if it feels like a step backward to you. No one takes care of you like your Mom. :) We wish you the best of luck in everything, Lorraine.

Warmly,

Denise & Pete

33

Next door to our gym was a yarn shop in which I'd seen older ladies gathered around tables, knitting and talking. A roomful of chatty grandmas seemed like a resource at least as valuable as hairdressers. My mom and her friends constantly gossiped about their kids and everyone else's too—I figured these ladies might know of a girl.

After months of putting it off, one morning in early November, I walked into the yarn shop. Handing the young girl at the register our flyer, I gave her my spiel and told her I was hoping to drop off some flyers for the women who came into the shop. She skimmed our letter.

"You need to talk to Jan," she said. "Come by Saturday morning."

I was hoping yarn-shop girl would say, *yeah, you can leave some flyers*, and I could check Yarn del Sol off my networking spreadsheet. But I'd worked retail and understood that leaving flyers by the register required manager approval, this Jan it sounded like, so I thanked the girl and left.

After spin on Saturday morning, I went back to the shop. Two long, oval tables of women sat knitting and chatting. They reminded me of Mom in their holiday-motif sweatshirts and sensible white sneakers. Honeycombed wooden shelves housed skeins of yarn, each cubby holding a different color. I told the girl at the register—a different girl than I'd spoken to before—that I was looking for Jan.

"There...with the white sweater," she said, with a nod toward the far end of the room.

Jan sat at the head of the table, talking with the women around her, shaking her head in amusement at something one of the women had said. Her silver-white hair was bobbed just above her shoulders, her body type pleasantly plump. I liked the look of her. I walked over to introduce myself.

"Hi, Jan? I'm Denise," I said, putting my hand out as she got up from the table. "My husband and I are hoping to adopt a baby, and I left a flyer here for you on Wednesday morning? I was hoping we could leave a few here and if any of the women heard of someone, they might be willing to pass our info along."

"Yes, I read your flyer, and I am so happy to meet you, Denise," she said. Without letting go of my hand, she placed her free hand, warm and dry, on top of our handshake and kept it there as she spoke.

"I have two adopted grandchildren, and I gave up a child for adoption when I was eighteen," she said.

I was taken aback that she would be so open—*so verbal* about having given up a baby. And in front of all the other women. The unexpected warmth of her reception and the candor with which she talked made me want to be open with her, too—to try to pay her back in part but also to rise to her level.

"I'm adopted, too," I said, though of course she knew that; she'd read our flyer.

"Have you ever talked to your birth mom?" she asked.

"No," I said. "It's not something that's ever been, uh, ... a burning desire of mine. I don't want to hurt my mom—my mom's just my mom, you know?"

"Of course," she said.

The son Jan placed for adoption had found her. He'd called when he was graduating from Duke with a degree in neuroscience.

"He called to thank me," she said. "We talked for ten minutes and decided that was all either of us really needed," she smiled with tears in her eyes. "But it was wonderful."

The woman to Jan's left broke into the conversation.

"My son and his wife are trying to adopt; they don't have *any* children yet," she told me, her mouth making a tight little line as she glanced at the photo of Jack and Kate smiling up at us from the flyer in my hand.

I got it. The fact that we were searching for a baby at the same time her son was placed us in direct competition. If Pete and I got a baby first, that would be the same as taking a baby away from her son and his wife. I felt the same way toward every couple featured in Alan's 'Adoptive Families Gallery.'

"They're being sent overseas for his job in six months, so if they don't get their baby soon it's not going to happen for them," she said with clipped irritation at my existence—my existence in her knitting circle and my existence as a barrier between her son and daughter-in-law's happiness.

Jan gently steered our bodies back around so the conversation was ours again. "Adoption is a beautiful thing; it's affected my life in so many ways," she said. "I'll do everything I can to help you find your baby." *Your baby.* Like our baby was a fact. Like she was out there, we just needed to find her.

As Jan and I hugged goodbye, hot tears ran down my face. When she felt my tears on her cheek and hugged me tighter, I had to choke back a sob. I was stinky, and sweaty, and clinging to this woman who ten minutes ago had been a stranger.

Why are you crying?

I couldn't put my finger on it.

34

The next morning, Pete and I had a date. Our favorite babysitter, Nadia—a young Mexican woman who'd been Kate's nursery school teacher—showed up with her Mary Poppins-like bag full of games, crafts, and baking supplies. When Nadia came to babysit, Jack and Kate were as happy to see us go as we were to be going. We were out the door by 8 a.m.

We drove to The Montage in Laguna Niguel. We couldn't afford to stay there, so we would crash as day guests. We walked through the lobby and stepped down into a room with a large fireplace framed with green, glazed Craftsman tiles and flanked by plump, down-filled couches. Perfectly chosen plein air pieces hung perfectly on the walls. Just beyond the piano, two-story, floor-to-ceiling glass doors opened to an unobstructed view of the Pacific. Sinking into the couches, you could hear the crackling of the fire and feel the crash of the surf in your chest.

We took the elevator to the restaurant upstairs so we could sit on the patio with a view of the ocean. We ordered breakfast the way we did only without kids: fresh squeezed orange juice, farmer's market fruit plate, eggs benedict, huevos rancheros, espresso. We'd picked up the LA Times, the New York Times, and USA Today to savor later on the couches, but for the moment, we set them aside.

"How are you feeling about the adoption?" Pete asked.

"I'm good," I said, taking a temperature-gauging sip of my latte. "I'm excited to talk at Precious Life—that she actually took me up on it, you know?"

"Why wouldn't she?" Pete said biting into a pastry. "You're adopted, you know more about adoption than anyone I know—you *should* be speaking about adoption. You do know none of the girls are going to give you their baby that day, though, right?" he said, swiping at his mouth with a white cloth napkin.

"Probably…but you never know; I'm *very* good," I flirted back.

We talked about his job. He was in sales. Sometimes when we'd lie in bed, he'd tell me he hated his job—the unrelenting pressure of *what've you done for me lately?* I didn't know what to say. I knew what he *wanted* me to say. He wanted me to say if he hated it that much, then he should quit. That I'd go back to work full-time. That we'd get by until he found something he liked better. Or, what he *really* wanted me to say was, "You stay home; it's your turn." Both of us wanted to be the stay-at-home parent, but in contradiction to my identity as a feminist, I felt I should stay home because I was The Mom. And because Pete was raised conservatively, and because he loved me, he signed off on the deal. So when we laid in bed and Pete told me he hated his job, I'd say, "Thank you for working so hard for us."

After breakfast, we walked out onto the back lawn. Pete took the path that wound down to the beach, and I sat in one of the Adirondack chairs that circled the fire pit. I kicked off my flip-flops and propped my feet on the stone hearth, letting the flames get hot on the soles of my feet. I closed my eyes and listened to the surf with my face to the sun. After a while, Pete came up behind me and put his hands on my shoulders. Pete's hands on my shoulders could communicate many things. A quick squeeze or two could mean, *Wrap it up; I'm ready to go.* A deeper massage type of effort could mean, *Sex today? Or maybe on Friday and you'll shave your legs?* But this touch was neither of those. It was faint but intentional. It said, *I remember who you are. I remember us.* We sometimes went weeks without touching like this. Months. There were days we went without making eye contact. The tears stung as they sprouted in the corners of my eyes.

The morning was slipping away. We'd told Nadia we'd be home around noon. As Pete turned onto PCH, I asked him to take the coast so we could milk the morning a little longer.

"Wouldn't it be great if we didn't have to go home?" I said, rolling down my window to breathe in the salt air. "If we could spend the whole day here, reading our papers by the fire and going from coffee to cocktails like we used to?"

"Yep. But we can't. We gotta get home to the crazy. And *you* want to add to it," he said with a conspiratorial smile.

11/9/2013 DBML sent to Hannah

35

I walked up the front steps of Precious Life shelter, a welcoming California bungalow.

Just inside the door, a young woman with a vaguely secretarial vibe sat at a desk. She pointed me to a row of rooms off the living room behind her.

Audrey's office was the size of a walk-in pantry. Scribbled, brightly colored Post-It Notes framed her monitor, and a picture of Audrey and a woman who, feature-wise, looked to be her grown daughter, sat in a cut-glass frame on her desk.

"Audrey?" I asked.

Audrey's spikey auburn hair conveyed a no-bullshit demeanor, which her New Jersey accent added to. "Denise. Glad you're here," she said. "The girls are just finishing lunch clean- up. I'll show you around."

There was a building set further back on the property that you couldn't see from the street, a dormitory the size of a small motel. Audrey took me in a few of the girls' rooms; they were sparse but clean and comfortable. Each had a bed and a crib, and the girls had added their own touches—lots of purple and neon, hearts and stuffed animals. In each room, there was a well-stocked basket of necessities: formula, baby wash, diapers, wipes and cream. I ached at the familiarity, the casual presence of newborns.

Audrey and I walked upstairs to the eating area—several tables in a large dining room, each with a cheerful silk sunflower centerpiece. She showed me the chore schedule posted in a Plexiglass frame on the wall. Each girl worked a rotation of cooking, cleaning, trash, etc.

"Once the baby's born, they have to have an outside job to stay here," she said. "They have to learn how to create a budget and stick to it. They pay rent, and they have to put a percentage in savings. If they can't or won't do these things, they can't stay."

I was impressed—the girls were more disciplined with their budgets than I was.

Finally, Audrey took me to the small classroom where I'd be talking to the girls. Two long rectangular tables had been pushed together, with chairs circled around.

"Speaker attendance is required as part of the girls' life skills classes," Audrey said. "So I expect a good turnout." I was pleased to be required. She pointed to an old projector case on the counter the size and shape of a Samsonite, "You know how to work it?"

"Yeah, I think so," I said, not wanting to sound incompetent before I'd even started. Audrey wished me luck and left the room.

I was wrestling with the cables, trying to get my laptop to sync with the projector, when the girls started filing in.

"I'm pretty good with computers; I can help you," one of the girls volunteered. She was Black, with braids past her shoulders, and big. Not big as in fleshy, big as in Serena Williams kick-your-ass, big.

"Shawntae has some *kaaaawl-edge*, so she know computers," one of the white girls taunted with a blaccent.

"Shut up," Shawntae answered, in a calm, dismissive manner that said she wasn't really bothered by the white girl.

As Shawntae performed tech support, I took in the group. There were three Black girls, four white. Two of the Black girls, including Shawntae, had their babies with them, sleeping soundly in their buckets. The other five girls were all in late pregnancy. One of the girls—a petite brunette, with doe-like brown eyes, expertly applied makeup, and a pristine and stylish outfit—reminded me of Minka Kelly in 'Friday Night Lights.'

Shawntae gave up and went back to her seat. I felt the weight of their stares as I unproductively pressed Fn and F1 over and over again.

"Screw it," I said. "Just pull your chairs behind me so you can see my screen." I'd purposely said "screw it," to show them my gritty side.

The girls pushed their chairs behind mine; Shawntae and another girl sat on either side of me. I began my PowerPoint. I showed them pictures: Mom and me on my wedding day; Mom, Dad, Bob and me outside the courtroom the day my adoption became official. In the photo, Mom's wearing a chic, navy blue shift with white trim; she holds me in her arms, beaming. I showed them the photo in the front yard with Cooper, and they all said, "Awww…" just the way I'd hoped—the way that told me they were seeing what was real: the joy and exuberance of Katie's personality, the fundamental sweetness of Jack's, the easy affection of arms around necks and hands resting on thighs. And maybe (hopefully?) they were seeing things that weren't true: a perfect marriage, a mom who didn't scream at her kids.

I went on to the next slide, 'How I Feel About Being Adopted.'

- Grateful to my birth mom
- I feel like my family was the family that I was meant to be with
- I am grateful for my secure, happy, childhood
- I think of my birth mom as a strong and brave woman

I was laying it on a little thick with that last bullet. I'd never thought of my birth mom as a hero, I thought of her as a regular high school girl. But I wanted *these* girls to feel empowered, to know that adoption could be a strong and brave choice. I wanted them to know this somewhat for their benefit but really for mine. I knew from the books and the classes that women considering placing their baby for adoption sometimes felt like they couldn't because they'd been made to feel that choosing adoption meant they were weak: *A real woman would raise her baby*, or worse, heartless: *How could you?* But women counseled to consider adoption as a brave choice, a loving choice, were more likely to place their babies and felt more confident in their decision.

I pulled up the next slide, 'Ways Adoption Has Changed Since I was Adopted'

- Almost all adoptions today are open—you choose what YOU want in regards to openness.
- You choose the family that will raise your baby
- Placing your baby is not goodbye forever—open adoption can be what you want (visits, pictures, etc.)
- Pregnancy-related expenses are paid for by the family you choose: medical care, prescriptions, rent, maternity clothes, groceries.

"It's cool you can pick parents for your baby," Shawntae said. "I never knew that."

The other girls nodded their heads in agreement. No one they knew had ever talked about adoption much. They had no idea they could still be involved in their babies' lives if that's what they wanted. I'd accomplished my professional goal, and I was happy to have done a good job for Audrey.

I put up the last slide: 'Questions?'

They wanted to know what kind of work I did that I was able to work from home. They wanted to know what Pete did. Then, Sara, the quiet, Mia Farrow wispy-blonde in the back, raised her hand.

"I'm adopted, and it was a horrible experience," she said. She didn't say it angrily; she just set the information on the table. But when she spoke again, she spoke with force, "My parents were really strict, and I never felt loved. I moved out when I was just sixteen, (*How old was she now—seventeen?*), and I would never put my baby through what I've been through."

SHIT. *Shit. Shit. Shit. Shit. Shit.* Shut up, Sara. *Shut. The Fuck. Up.*

Sara's words sucked all of the goodwill toward me, toward adoption in general, out of the room. And as much as I wanted one of those girls to give me their baby, if they didn't but walked out of there thinking of adoption as a positive thing? I was feeling pretty good about that. But Sara had torpedoed me. Her experience was definitely *not* on message. But her pain was real.

And she was young enough to be my daughter.

I turned my chair around to face her, "I'm so sorry that happened to you. My experience of being adopted was a very good one, and yours was a very bad one, and I'm sorry. Do you still talk to your parents?"

"I could, but I don't want to…" she said with a shrug.

One of the other girls jumped in with, "What'd you have to do for the home study?" and we moved on.

When it was time to go, Georgia, a gangly white girl in baggy, orange hoop shorts, who I would've sworn was a lesbian, stood up, put her hands on her hips, and said matter-of-factly, "Whelp, I'm not considering adoption, but if I was, I would totally pick you guys," and I laughed out loud because, while I wasn't gettin' Georgia's baby, I appreciated her vote of confidence. Her proclamation physically released me—like someone had unpinned my shoulders from a clothes line. The pressure was off; my pitch was done. I thanked Georgia and hugged her goodbye.

Shawntae's son, Owen, had woken up, and I was holding him when Minka Kelly came up and asked, "Can I have one of your letters? I'm due in two weeks."

"Yeah…of course," I said, trying to nonchalantly scramble a DBML out of my bag. I put our letter in her hands, and she slipped out the door.

11/14/2013 DBML sent to Kaitlin

36

We'd explained to the kids that they were getting a baby brother or sister, but we didn't know when—it could be next week, it could be next year. We told them another woman would grow the baby in her tummy, but she would give us her baby and it would be ours forever. Jack understood and was rooting for a brother. Kate was three, and it was unclear how much was sinking in.

The week before Thanksgiving, Kate's teacher, Mrs. Miranda—a petite, impeccably- dressed woman who spoke with the singsong inflection of a preschool teacher—was doing a unit on families. She had the kids make puppets to represent their family members. They chose from photocopied figures, colored them in, cut them out, and glued them onto Popsicle sticks.

At pick up, Mrs. Miranda sang out to me, smiling: "Miss Dee-neese, Kate chose her family all by herself—we did not help."

I took Kate's hand and we walked down the speckled linoleum hallway, out the metal double doors, and into the sunshine.

"Mama," she said, pulling on my hand, "Stop, I wanna show you."

I steered us off the sidewalk and over to the grass so we could sit—this clearly wasn't going to wait for the car. Kate opened an envelope and began taking out her puppets, laying them carefully on the grass.

"Here's Jacky. Here's Dada. Here's you, Mama," she said. "And here's our new baby!"

She'd chosen a baby in footie pajamas, which she'd colored pink. *She got it.* She understood that the baby coming *someday* would be her brother or sister (looked like she was pulling for sister), just like Jack was her brother. I had the sensation someone was squeezing my heart with their hand. She was more than okay with it; she was excited. She'd made our baby Popsicle stick official.

The Friday before Thanksgiving, after the kids had gone to bed, Pete and I made gin and tonics and settled in for a night of TV. Navigating to the most recent episode of 'Homeland,' out of the silence Pete said, "I think our baby's coming soon—I've just had that feeling lately."

"Really?" I said, not making eye contact for fear of asking too much from the moment and losing it altogether.

Pete's offering was a big deal. He didn't say things to give false hope. He didn't agree to go along. He said things of the mystical nature exactly never. So, when he said he thought our baby was coming soon, that he just had *that feeling?* I felt I could take his words as a promise. Hold them cupped in my hands like tea leaves.

"I've felt the same way," I told him.

11/22/2013 DBML sent to Sheila

37

The kids had the week of Thanksgiving off. Late one afternoon, we were making turkey cake pops that, at the time, I thought maybe I'd made up in my head but for sure saw in a magazine or online. We used candy corn for the feathers, candy eyes, and a snippet of Red Vines for the wattle. They weren't turning out as we'd hoped. The cake balls were heavy, so instead of being cute little turkeys perched atop a stick, the turkeys slid midway down, impaled. The eyes weren't staying put; they melted down the turkeys' faces, giving a surrealist effect.

We were mid-production when I got a call from a 503 number. Unfamiliar with the area code, my heart slammed into my ribcage.

"Hello?" I said.

"Hi. Uh...I'm pregnant. And, um...a friend of mine showed me your post on Facebook."

"Hi! We're really happy you're calling us," I said, stealing Tracey's line and wiping the melted chocolate from my hands onto a blue dishtowel.

I ran-walked to Pete's office. Jabbing my index finger at my phone, I wide-mouthed, "BIRTH-MOM! BIRTH-MOM!" I waved him toward the kitchen to take over kids and cake pops.

"Wow. You heard about us on Facebook? From who?"

"A friend of a friend of mine saw your guys' post."

Walking upstairs to our bedroom, I shut the door behind me and sat on the edge of the bed to concentrate on the girl from 503.

"What's your name? Where are you?" I asked.

"Jennifer. And I'm in St. Helens, Oregon," she said.

The Pacific Northwest. *Home.* St. Helens was just south of Longview, the town where I was born.

"I'm three months along," she said. And then we disconnected.

I frantically tried to call her back but got a motel. How could I've dialed a wrong number when I'd pressed redial? The clerk told me the call had come from a guest staying at the motel.

And that's when I understood that Jennifer was living out of the motel. And I didn't know her last name to ask for her room.

She called back a few seconds later.

"Sorry 'bout that. Anyway. My mom left when I was ten, and I bounced around foster care until I was finally adopted at seventeen," she said. "There's no way I'm telling the baby's dad about the baby or about giving it up for adoption."

"Okay," I said, knowing that wouldn't fly with Alan, but that now wasn't the time to bring that up with Jennifer.

"My pregnancy's high-risk," she said, "My doctor said the umbilical cord's grown into the placenta—probably cuz I got pregnant again too soon; I have a baby that's five months. He said I gotta get steroid shots once a week for the next fifteen weeks, to help the baby."

In the motel room in my mind, with 1970s goldenrod curtains and a matching quilted bedspread, a five-month-old baby appeared.

I asked for the name of her doctor and clinic, knowing Alan would want to confirm the pregnancy and see how high-risk it was before we proceeded. I was getting better at this. She gave the name of her doctor and clinic without hesitation.

"I'm due on May 23rd, but my doctor wants to schedule a C-section for fifteen weeks from now," she said. "I'm goin' in for an ultrasound tomorrow, so I'll know the sex then."

I didn't have a Birthmother Telephone Information Sheet with me. I squeezed my eyes shut to make the questions appear.

"There are some pretty intrusive questions I need to ask you, stuff our lawyer will want to know," I said.

"Fine, yeah. Go ahead," she said.

"How old are you?" I asked.

"Twenty-seven," she answered.

"What race are you?" I asked, feeling like a racist for asking.

"White," she said.

"Do you have other kids, besides the five-month-old?" I asked.

"Yeah, I have a two-year-old, too," she said.

A sweet, two-year-old boy in need of a haircut popped into the frame, sitting on the bedspread beside her.

"Do you have any Native American in your blood, in your heritage?" I asked.

"Yeah, my biological grandfather is full-blooded Cherokee," she said.

Shit.

When a baby's heritage includes Native American, the Indian Childhood Welfare Act (ICWA) changes the adoption process in two ways. First, the birth mom, or the tribe elders, can change their minds up until the adoption is finalized (at which point, the baby will typically have been with you for nine months to a year); and secondly, the tribe must be invited to attend all court dates, including finalization day.

The need for the ICWA is undeniable. From 1860, up until as recently as 1970, the US government ripped Native American children from their families and put them in 'Indian

Schools' and foster homes, forcing them to assimilate. The children had to give up their names and were assigned English ones. Their spiritual beliefs were mocked, and they were forced to adopt Christianity. Speaking in their languages was forbidden, even to each other. The teachers often mocked their Native American students and taught them that their culture was inferior.

I supported the ICWA unequivocally. But, knowing that if we began the process of adopting a Native American baby—an adoption the biological mother and father both wanted— that the tribe would still have the final word, that the baby I'd held and kissed and mothered for a year could be taken from me on what was meant to be finalization day? It was the absolute worst-case scenario. Pursuing the adoption of a Native American baby wasn't out of the question, but it was a path that Alan had warned us against.

"Have you talked to other families about possibly adopting your baby?" I asked Jennifer.

"Oh yeah. I had one couple all picked out," she said. "They didn't have kids, and they seemed really nice, and then they got all freaked out about my pregnancy being high-risk and they were telling me what to eat and what to do, so I just told them, no. I mean *I was giving them my baby*, and they're trying to tell me what to do?" She took a breath. "So then I picked out these two gay guys. They were really sweet in the beginning, but then they wanted me to take all these vitamins and get even more steroid shots, so I told them no way. *I mean, I was giving them my baby* and they were acting all ungrateful and shit."

My heart sank. Even if Jennifer chose us, I knew it'd only be a matter of time before we did something to offend her and she'd be telling some other couple about why she'd dropped us. But it was still thrilling. Maybe it would work out.

"We're very interested in adopting your baby. I need to talk to Pete and our lawyer, but I promise I'll call you back tomorrow," I said.

She gave me her room number, and we hung up.

I called Alan and told him the things I knew about Jennifer: the high-risk pregnancy, the Cherokee grandfather, that she was set on not telling the father.

"Denise," he said, "This is an undesirable situation for any one of those reasons you listed. Put all together, along with the fact that she's already dumped two sets of adoptive parents, I strongly advise you not to move forward with her."

I was livid.

Was he just going to say no to everyone? Because all of the books said you couldn't wait for the "perfect" situation to come along—you had to work through some messy stuff. You had to work with the birth mom, to convince her to tell the father. You had to write to the Cherokee Nation, to see if they wanted the child; maybe they wouldn't. You had to hope that her pregnancy would go near full-term. It wasn't supposed to be easy. Alan had told us it was our job to go out and find a birth mom, and that's exactly what I'd done. I'd brought him Eileen in August, and he'd called that opportunity a ham half-off. Now I'd brought him Jennifer, and he was saying this opportunity wasn't right for us either? Why was I doing all of this fucking work if it was catch and release?

38

We didn't move forward with Jennifer. I knew Alan was right, but I was down, disheartened. The holidays had arrived and I thought we'd be building a relationship with a birth mom by then. The most discouraging part was that we'd had a lot of contact—it felt like *something* should've come of it. As I lay in bed the pre-dawn hours of Thanksgiving, I considered each situation, each woman, moving from one to the next like fingers on worry beads:

- Eileen from Las Cruces: she'd been raped twice, and her baby girl had tested positive for cocaine and been taken into custody by CPS. Where was her baby? She'd be five months old now.
- Gina and her inner-city nurse hook-up: another family had claimed the baby before we'd even had a chance to raise our hand.
- Marcia's friend, Anita: the MBA-holding, successful, divorced mom of two grown kids had started over with her new baby boy.
- Texas Jennifer: the Chili's bartender with two kids, a restraining order, and nowhere to live. She hadn't called again after the windy phone call. Did she get an abortion?
- Tara from Vegas: she'd questioned the love I'd have for my adopted baby— surely that meant other birth moms were passing on us for the same reason.

- Patty's friend, Laura: another older, professional, divorced woman. After that first breathless conversation, we'd never spoken about Laura again; that'd been two months ago. She was probably keeping her baby.
- Oregon Jennifer: High-risk, quarter-Cherokee Jennifer who'd ditched two families. I pictured her and her babies in their motel room.

After all of the contact, all of the opportunities, only one still existed: Lorraine. She was a full-time student, working a full-time job. She was close to her family. She'd never voiced concern about us having biological children—her adoptive parents had biological children too; it made her a unique and perfect fit for us. She may've had Gemma with one man, been going through a divorce with another, and be pregnant with still another man's baby, but Lorraine was the fresh-faced ingénue in our story. It had to be her.

The last email I'd sent her was on November 1, after the second missed Skype, after she hadn't picked up the paperwork. I'd wished her "the best of luck in everything." It was a passive aggressive move. I wondered: Did I let my pride get in the way? If she decided to place her baby, did she know we'd still come running?

November 27, 2013

Hello and Happy Thanksgiving

Hi Lorraine,

I woke up in the middle of the night last night and could not get back to sleep because I was thinking about you, so I knew I wanted to write you a note. How are you? How is your baby boy doing? How is living at home? Is it nice to have Mom and Dad taking care of you, or do you long to be on your own? (You don't have to answer all of these questions!)

We wanted to tell you so that you don't have any doubts that we would be honored and thrilled to parent and love your baby. I don't know where you're at in the decision to place him for adoption, but we wanted you to know that we are still here for you. When we were talking and Skyping, it was a rollercoaster for us when you wouldn't show up, but we both understand the need to shut out the world sometimes and just think.

We adore you and think you are a strong woman. We wish you the happiest Thanksgiving, Lorraine!

Hugs,
Denise & Pete

November 30, 2013

Hi Denise,

I've been so busy with doctor appointments, Christmas shopping, starting a new job, and taking care of my daughter. Tomorrow will mark my 32 weeks of pregnancy, and he is just growing like a tree!!! I didn't think you all wanted to talk to me anymore since the last time I missed Skyping with you all. I didn't mean to do that, just had so much going on, and I should've let you all know. I hope you had a great Thanksgiving. I am still in the process of what to do with this baby boy growing inside of me. I want to do adoption. It just seems like the right thing to do, but the father is trying to fight me on this now! I don't know why this is, but my parents and I are going to talk to a lawyer sometime this next week to see what my options are. I'm sorry again for the late responses as well as missing our Skype dates. You and Pete are definitely my pick if I'm able to get the father to agree!

Lorraine

If she placed her baby for adoption, we would be his parents! And she and her parents were going to see a lawyer—that showed a level of seriousness Lorraine hadn't shown before (Thank god the adults were finally stepping in.).

She was probably telling Jared one story, and us another, but one of them had to be true. And if I was super-supportive adoptive mom, maybe I could lead her farther down my path than Jared could his. I was sure that if he convinced Lorraine to keep their baby, he'd be gone within the year. Lorraine's descriptions of Jared as, "texting me mean things," and "being just crazy," so much so that she'd moved back in with her parents to, "get away from his craziness," made me angry. And nervous. I pictured him in baggy jeans, a spotless white t-shirt hanging loosely on his willowy frame, a thick silver chain around his neck. I imagined him making her pregnant heart swoon with tales of how tight their little family was going to be, and then after, as he wiped his dick off on her parent's bathroom towel, yelling over his shoulder that he was going out for a while. I never once considered that Jared might want to parent his son, that he might love Lorraine, or that he was a good guy. He was a one-dimensional rival.

Lorraine and her parents were meeting with a lawyer the following Friday, December 6.

She wanted us to resend the paperwork to get things started, and she wanted to meet in person. "My family and I would love to meet you all before the baby comes!" she wrote. "I think it would be an awesome idea just so that I can see how everything works out face to face!"

She was due in eight weeks.

December 8, 2013

Hi Lorraine,

How did the meeting with the lawyer go? Did you pick up our letter from Alan? Let us know where you are in your thought process for the adoption and how things went with the lawyer. We have been thinking of you, wondering how it went and how you are--I know talking to a lawyer isn't really something anyone wants to do.

Hugs,

Denise & Pete

December 10, 2013

Hi Denise,

Got your package today! That's some paperwork, for sure. :-) I finished most of it, but I have a few things I need to finish. The father of the baby is going to make this very difficult, so I'm just praying for the best. He's only thinking about himself and being selfish! I wish he would just agree and make it that much easier.

Are we gonna fight him, Lorraine? We'll give him all we've got, okay? You and me, girl.

Or am I the only one fighting, throwing punches in the air?

39

The French doors were open to the cool night air. At six o'clock, neighbors began walking in with hostess gifts, trays of mini-quiche, and balls of cranberry-covered goat cheese. Pete made sure everyone got a drink while I ushered kids upstairs, pointing them toward the Wii. By six-thirty, Pandora had to be cranked up, the food table was overflowing, and the thumps of knees and elbows from upstairs told us the kids had settled in. Our Christmas party had successfully launched.

We'd been in the house just over a year, and there were a couple of neighbors I didn't know well but wanted to, like Julie—the home-school mom of what appeared to be a ton of kids, five doors down. I liked the chunky necklaces she wore. Her kids were polite, addressing Pete and me as Mr. and Mrs. Massar. And they weren't cookie-cutter kids. They didn't play soccer; they did Irish Dance. They didn't have straight hair but unwieldy brown ringlets.

Julie read our adoption flyer I'd put in her hands.

"I didn't know it was done like this," she said, sounding both baffled and impressed. "This is amazing. I'd love to help you guys…I'll spread the word."

I'd forgotten that stumping for a baby was a new concept to most people. It'd been a new and distasteful concept to me just seven months earlier. But the unsavoriness of trying to sniff out a birth mom among friends of friends no longer fazed me. Like those marathon runners who have menstrual blood or shit running down their legs, I was running toward the finish line without embarrassment or self-consciousness.

Around eight-thirty, the liquor table needed restocking. I went into the kitchen to grab mixers, ice, and wine. As I walked by the microwave nook, the dump area where we charged our phones, I saw I had an incoming call from Emily. My heart jumped. A call from Emily didn't mean a baby, only a call from Alan could mean baby, but still, this was something if she was calling on a Friday night.

Plugging one ear with my middle finger and pressing my phone to the other, I spoke over the party noise but tried not to yell, "Hello?"

"Hi, Denise. It's Emily. From Lullaby."

"Yeah. Hi, Emily! What's up?" I answered, trying to wedge myself into the three-inch space between the microwave and the fridge.

"Your out-of-state clearance came through today," she said. "I just found out this evening and knew you and Pete would want to know right away."

After thanking Emily and hanging up, I walked down into the den where Pete was talking to a horseshoe of husbands whose names I'd been given earlier but already forgotten. I cupped my hands around his ear: "EMILY JUST CALLED. OUR CLEARANCE FROM IOWA CAME THROUGH!"

Raising his beer, Pete announced to the horseshoe: "We just got a clearance we've been waiting for in our adoption."

"Excellent!" they said, raising plastic cups and brown bottles to our good news.

If someone calls us with a baby tonight, we can go and get her.

For real.

40

By the following Tuesday, Lorraine had had the paperwork—the documents that would start the adoption process in earnest—for a week.

December 17, 2013

Hi Lorraine,

How's it going? Were you able to get the paperwork completed? You have been on our minds. We'd love to know how you are.

XO, Denise & Pete

December 19, 2013

Denise,

Paperwork will be done by tonight and mailed out tomorrow morning :-) It's a lot of questions and things I had to ask to find out as well. No worries though; it will be completely finished tonight after work and then mailed out!!!

Lorraine

I smiled at her smiley face. There was no mention of Jared. The paperwork was going out tonight.

41

Bob and his longtime-girlfriend, Stephanie, lived in Kuna, a small town outside of Boise, in a sprawling house with their four teenagers, a Doberman, a teacup Yorkie, and a calico cat.

Mom lived less than a mile away in a cozy three-bedroom house. When we visited, we stayed with her, setting up camp unselfconsciously: sleeping bags, clothes, sippy cups strewn. Mom stocked her house with chocolate milk and sugar cereal, and when the kids woke at 5:45 a.m., wanting cartoons and Eggo's, she'd already be padding around the kitchen in her housecoat making coffee like she wouldn't have it any other way.

I'd fantasized about my family prodding us over dinner, *"So...how's the adoption going?"* Mom knew vaguely of Lorraine, but Bob and Stephanie didn't know anything. All eyes on us, we'd drop the highlight reel, "Due in less than a month...pretty constant contact...vet school." But no one prodded. No one asked us anything about the adoption. I could've volunteered information about Lorraine. That's what healthy, well-adjusted adults do when they want to talk about something, right, they bring it up? Not my family. We prefer to hold desperately longed-for conversations with ourselves and in our heads.

"If they're not gonna *ask*, I'm not gonna tell them," I told Pete as we crawled onto the tall blow-up with the slow leak in Mom's guest room.

Earlier in December, Bob had called, telling me they were planning a surprise night out for the adults. He'd sent menu options and told us to pack warm clothes. The night of the surprise, Bob wound his Durango, holding Stephanie, Mom, Pete and me up the icy hairpin turns of Bogus Basin Mountain, the view over the dark, sheer cliffs making my armpits prickle. The only thing at the top of the mountain was the ski lodge. I was disappointed. Having dinner in the lodge would be fun for Bob and me—reliving so many Saturdays of our childhood, eating steaming chili out of paper cups, breathing air heavy with the scent of wet wool—but it wouldn't be an easy walk for Mom, and there was no nostalgic hook for Pete. But as we crested the mountain, Bob drove past the lodge, past the chairlift lights casting circles on the snow. Snow crunching under our tires, he continued on a dark mountain road that stretched beyond the lodge. We parked at a large cabin and joined the group gathered out front. The sky full of stars, Pete and I watched the moisture in our breath freeze into tiny clouds.

I heard them before I saw them—two teams of Clydesdales trotting out of the woods pulling sleighs. I was horse crazy in grade school. I took riding lessons and stayed after to pick hooves and muck stalls to be near them. I loved the smell of the alfalfa and grain, the feel of their muzzles under my lips and nose, silken and prickly. I bought a yellow plastic sweat scraper at the tack shop because it was the cheapest grooming tool they had, and I wanted to own something a real horsewoman would own. Bob had borne witness, and he was betting that somewhere inside of me the thrill of being near a horse still existed. And he was right. I was warmed by the reminder: My family knew me; they knew everything and everyone I'd ever loved.

We glided along a wide path cut through the trees, the bells on the leather harnesses jingle-jangling with the horses' footfall. The drivers pulled the teams to a stop in front of a log cabin, smoke rising from its chimney. The two groups unloaded and we made our way inside where rows of wooden tables stretched the length of the room and a fire crackled at the back of the cabin. We took a table and were quickly served ice-cold beer in sweaty bottles. We related to each other in a way we didn't when we sat at our own dining room tables. Pete and Mom's laughter was real. Stephanie was relaxed and talkative. I had no agenda for the conversation.

Between courses, cowboys got up and read their cowboy poetry and made corny jokes that, on another night, would have been too downhome for my taste. But on that night I laughed until I had tears in my eyes because they were good at what they did, the evening was perfect, and family was everything.

As the horses carried us back to our cars, the group was quiet, sated and sleepy. As we glided along, I watched great chunks of snow slough away from the tall pines and crash to the ground. A light, new snow began to fall.

> 12/26/2013 DBML sent to Trina

42

We were back home on December 27. The last email I'd sent Lorraine was on December 20, which she hadn't responded to.

December 27, 2013

Hi Lorraine,

We wanted to wish you a Merry Christmas and a Happy New Year. We spent the last week in Boise with my family, and we thought of you often and wondered what you were doing.

How was your Christmas? How are you? You are in your last month now--are you comfortable, or are you ready to be done?

Hugs,

Denise & Pete

December 29, 2013

Denise,
I'm so ready for it to be the due date already! I'm hoping everything goes as planned as well. It's looking now like he is

trying to fight because he wants his son. He has the right to his son, but I just don't think he's ready for that kind of commitment yet. He has no idea what's in store at this point. Three more weeks till my due date as of today. Did you get the paperwork yet? I gave it to my mom to look over, and then she said she would send it, but I'm not sure if anything was sent yet? My dad says he thinks the baby will be here by January 15th; what are your guys' guesses? He's due on the 26th, but he's full term as of next Sunday, the fifth. That's okay with me if he comes any time after that or on that day, lol.

Lorraine

"It's looking now like he is trying to fight because he wants his son. He has the right to his son I just don't think he's ready for that kind of commitment yet."

His son. His son.

"Did you get the paperwork yet? I gave it to my mom to look over and then she said she would send it, but I'm not sure if anything was sent yet?"

We were never getting the paperwork.

"My dad says he thinks baby will be here by January 15, what are your guys' guesses?"

Playing this game will break our hearts. Stop. Please stop.

It was there in the way she knew exact dates, "I am 35.5 weeks pregnant today," and "He will be full term on Sunday the 5th." I knew the deep satisfaction of milestones; I felt it when I carried Jack and Kate, announcing to Pete, "He's as big as a plum!" or "She's a grapefruit this week!" It'd been there, too, in her tenderness of voice when she'd written and spoken of him.

I knew she didn't want to hurt my feelings, didn't want to tell me that she'd just been curious—that she'd never meant for it to get this far. I'd allowed it to go on. I'd *forced* it to go on. She'd broken contact, and then at Thanksgiving, with no other possibilities on the horizon, I'd pulled her back in. She didn't have the heart then to tell me I hadn't found my baby. That I needed to start over. That this baby boy was hers.

Somebody needed to end the performance—the forty-year-old woman needed to. I wrote my response feeling a mash-up of emotions. I was sad to let go of the only birth mom we were talking to. I was angry at her for leading us on. I was embarrassed I'd let her. I was mad at myself for trying to force a relationship without anything real at the core. But it also felt good to finally emerge as the grown-up, to stop living as a shapeshifter in the world of LOLs and smiley faces and speak the truth.

December 29, 2013

Hi Lorraine,

Our lawyer has not received the paperwork yet. We are here for you and would be so honored to raise and love your baby and give him everything we can to make his life secure and happy. But at this point, the paperwork should have been completed, and we should be working together with your lawyer and our lawyer on a legal adoption plan. It sounds like you may be considering raising the baby with the baby's dad. We totally understand your desire to do that and would never want to discourage you. To protect our hearts, we need to know that you are committed to placing your baby in our family. If not, then communicating about the baby, etc., is not fair to you or us.

Much Love,

Denise & Pete

> 12/30/2013 DBML sent to Nicole

FINDING

43

My phone rang at 6 a.m.

What kind of asshole calls at 6 a.m. on New Year's Day?

At 6:02, Pete's phone rang, and that's when I went cold. Our moms were older, and I was sure that a 6 a.m. call to both of us meant one of them was in the hospital or worse. Pete got out of bed and jogged downstairs to get his phone.

I lay perfectly still to discern the tone of his response, but he said nothing more than *Hello?* before falling silent, listening to the person on the other end who was apparently talking non-stop. I sat up and tilted my head toward the door. I heard Pete coming back up, his footsteps steady on the carpeted stairs. Still not a word. He walked into our bedroom, smiling, phone to his ear. He came around to my side of the bed, an oddly intimate gesture, moving the phone away from his mouth but not his ear.

"There's a baby for us," he said.

"Shut up. No, there's not. Not really," I said. I grabbed the phone, thinking there was a very good chance Pete had misunderstood.

"Alan? It's Denise. We have a baby?"

"Good morning, Denise," Alan answered in his taffy-pull cadence. "Yes, you and Peter have a son. He is waiting for you to pick him up."

I looked at Pete with one hand over my mouth, tears streaming, nodding and nodding—

You were right! You were right!

"Denise, you need to grab a pencil," Alan said. "I'm going to give you a lot of information, and you need to write it all down."

We ran downstairs to the dining room table, Pete grabbing a pad and pen as I laid the phone on the table and put Alan on speaker.

"Ready," I said.

"Your son was born on New Year's Eve. His birth mom chose you and Peter from the hospital, and she and the birth father would both like to meet you. You need to be at the hospital by this afternoon or evening at the latest. When you land, you and Peter will drive to her lawyer's office. Don is my colleague we sent your Dear Birth Mom Letters to—remember him? Yes. Well, he will walk you through the paperwork and then take you to the hospital to meet your son."

"Should I take the time to shower and look decent or should we just *get there*?"

Of course I needed to take a shower. I couldn't walk into our birth mom's hospital room all bedhead and morning breath, but Alan was stressing *time*, and there was a baby waiting for me to pick him up and introduce myself as his mama, and my instinct was to jump in the car, drive to John Wayne airport, throw our credit cards at the first agent we saw, *AND GET THERE*.

"Yes, get presentable. But do hurry," Alan replied. "I have a few documents I want you to read before you meet your birth mom; I'll send them while you're in the air, and you can read them on the drive to Don's office. Oh, and make sure you bring a car seat."

Jack and Kate. They were asleep in their beds. They couldn't go with us, and we didn't have family nearby to come and take over. Except, we did. I called Mari's cell. No answer. I called the house phone.

Erik croakily answered, "Hello?"

"Erik, it's Denise. We have a baby! And we need to go get him. I need to talk to Mar."

"No shit?" Erik replied, still groggy, but I could hear the smile in his voice,

"Congratulations, you guys. Okay, okay, here she is."

"Mar, we got a baby. A baby boy."

"Oh my god."

"We have to be in Central California by this afternoon. Can you come and get the kids? We should just be gone this one night, but honestly, I don't know."

"Yes, yeah...for sure. I got it. Don't worry. Do I have time to shower, or should I just come?"

"Just come."

"Okay, I'll be there as fast as I can."

"Thank you. I love you. Bye."

"Love you, too."

Pete was online looking at flights.

"None of these flights get us there before two o'clock. I could drive us there faster than that," he said.

I ran back upstairs, stripping off my t-shirt and PJ bottoms, considering how good it would feel to get in the car and make immediate forward motion toward our baby, but knew instantly that driving was a bad idea. Pete would never be able to get there fast enough for me, and we'd both be a bundle of nerves. If we got lost? My god. I was trying to figure out how to say that without pissing him off, when he yelled upstairs, "Never mind...found a flight out of John Wayne that works. We need to leave in an hour—can you be ready?"

"Book it!" I yelled, getting in the shower.

Getting ready, I pulled my hair back into a wet ponytail but blew out the front pieces, so I looked done from straight on. Quickie make-up. I wanted to look as good as I could; I was worried that when our birth mom saw me, she'd be disappointed, think I was too old. She'd obviously seen our DBML, and those pictures had been taken within the last year, but I'd taken care with my hair and make-up for those photos. I liked to think that I looked mid-thirties in those pictures, not *forty*. I was afraid she was going to see me and change her mind.

While Pete showered, I packed. *I need to pack baby things.* I grabbed those newborn Pampers that smelled deliciously of baby powder. I brought down a few bottles and a container of formula. I chose a light blue sleeper with brightly colored trucks that Jack had worn. I didn't bring out the gauzy swaddling blankets that had been Kate's, though I planned on using them. I didn't want our birth mom to see that we'd be using hand-me-down pink blankets from his sister. I thought she might take offense that we hadn't bought all new things for her baby and change her mind. I gazed at the items across our bedspread, thrilled at their sudden legitimacy.

I threw clothes, jammies, toothbrushes, and a few toys into an overnight bag for Jack and Kate. We told them only that we were going to meet a woman who might want to give us her baby. They were excited to be going to Aunt Mari's. I'd never felt more grateful for her than I did that morning as we transferred car seats from my car to hers, and together we buckled my kids into her care—this girl I'd met on the cruise ship because we both liked smoking cigarettes and drinking hot chocolate in the officer's bar. Twenty years later, we were like sisters, and I was giving her my kids, unsure when I'd be back.

John Wayne was fifteen minutes from our house without traffic, and at 9 a.m. on New Year's Day, we were sailing. I felt weightless. It was the first time I'd sat still since we'd gotten the call.

"What are we gonna name him? Are we going with Harry?" I asked.

We'd talked about naming our baby, if it was a boy, after Pete's Grandpa. Grandpa Harry had served in the first paratrooper division of the U.S. Army, the 82nd Airborne, during WWII. He was an American hero, and he'd been good to Pete.

"I don't think I can pull the trigger," Pete said. "Kids might tease him and call him Hairy Assar."

"You think so?" I said, surprised but wondering then if our child *would* be called Hairy Assar. "I don't really think so, but it's your call. It's your grandpa."

"What about Henry?" I asked. Pete lifted the turn signal and turned right off MacArthur into the airport. "If we do Henry, we could do Harrison as his middle name as a tribute to Grandpa Harry."

"Yeah…" Pete said absently, trying it out in his head. "Yes. Henry," he said. "Henry Harrison Massar. I like it."

"Henry Harrison Massar," I spoke in confirmation.

We had a little time before our flight, so I wanted to get something for our birth mom, but options were limited: A stuffed animal? Candy? An 'I ♥ Orange County' hoodie? None carried anywhere near the sentiment I was looking for. I finally settled on a letter D key ring. It was inlaid with pink rhinestones and had some weight to it; it was a nice one. I know what you're thinking: *Good God, a key chain?!* I know. I know! But she and I shared the same first initial. And I thought that on the way to the hospital, we'd stop and get her a big bouquet of flowers, and I'd tie the D into the center of the bow. And I hoped the sparkly pink D might say: *"We have the same first initial, and that pleases me. I hope it pleases you. We'll be connected forever, you and I. I'll never be able to thank you enough, but…thank you."* I hoped the sparkly pink D might convey at least some of that.

With key chain tucked in the diaper bag, Pete and I arrived at our gate. Everything in me wanted to send Mom, or Amber, or Marcia a text saying, "GUESS WHERE I AM AND GUESS WHAT I'M DOING???!!!" But Pete and I had agreed we wouldn't tell anyone. Pete didn't want to tell people for practical reasons—the disappointment we'd feel if it didn't work out, plus having to let everyone *know* it hadn't worked out, would be too much. I felt the same and had the added sense that telling anyone outside of Mari and Erik would jinx it. We sat holding hands, waiting for our row to be called.

As I followed Pete down the aisle, I couldn't stop smiling. Antsy and smug, I felt as if I were flying to meet a lover. No, not just a lover, but someone I was falling in love with. I slung the blue diaper bag across my body messenger-style so that the mass of it lay over my belly and pressed it to me.

44

Heading to Don's office, I pulled out my phone to read the documents Alan had sent while we were in the air. An email titled: Interaction Letter—READ ME FIRST held a list of recommendations on how to handle things that might arise in the hospital. I read aloud as Pete drove.

Regarding what to say to the birth mom about the baby once it's born:
"Clients usually ask what they should say to the birth mother about the baby once it's born. They worry that if they gush too much about how beautiful the baby is, the birth mother will want to keep the baby. In fact, birth mothers find enthusiastic and complimentary remarks about their baby to be reaffirming of their good work. Some of the most effective remarks you might make could be along the lines of, 'She has your beautiful eyes,' or 'She has the sweetest smile.' You may feel free to say the baby is simply the most beautiful baby you've ever seen."

I was immensely grateful for Alan's counsel here. I'd thought about the hospital room conversation with our birth mom many times. What would I say to her as I held her baby in my arms? Should I play it cool? If I showed the birth mom how much I wanted her baby, wouldn't she want to keep it—

wasn't that just human nature? Should I tell her how beautiful and perfect her baby was? I didn't want to *sell her* on her baby. I was grateful for Alan's permission, encouragement even, to gush.

Regarding the Nursing Staff:
"At the hospital, whenever there is a shift change, you should introduce yourselves to the nurse on duty, and to the nurse charged with your birth mother's care to let him or her know who you are and where you're going to be. If you decide to spend the night at a local hotel or go out for half an hour to get something to eat, you should let your birth mother know where you are going and offer to bring back food from a local restaurant. Many of my clients find it very effective to stop at the nurse's station on their way out the door to see if the nursing staff would like the client to make a run to the local fast-food restaurant for hamburgers, salads or the like. The amount of goodwill engendered by making the offer cannot be overstated."

I was grateful for this counsel, too. I'd always excelled at ingratiating myself with authority figures, so making friends with the nurses was a no-brainer. But I found the suggestion that we might ask our birth mom if she wanted us to get her food comforting. Like maybe we wouldn't be walking on eggshells the whole time—that her actually giving us her baby might become so plausible that at some point it wouldn't seem obscene for Pete to say, "Anybody need a burger?"

Regarding Spending Time with Your Baby:
"The birth mother should get the sense from the nursing staff that either or both of you are in the nursery bonding with the baby every minute. There's nothing that upsets a birth mom more than hearing that the adoptive parents are somewhere other than with the baby in the nursery."

This one wasn't going to be a problem. I was going to hold the baby every second I could. I feared there would be excruciating moments, hours (*days*?) in which the birth mom would ask to be alone with her baby, and I'd spend that time convinced she was changing her mind. (That happened a lot on 'I'm Having Their Baby.' When the birth mom requested alone time with the baby, it never ended well for the adoptive parents.) Pete and I would stay at the hospital as late as we were allowed and be back half an hour before visitors were welcome in the morning.

I turned to Pete. "How long can I hold him before you want a turn?"

"You take all the time you want," he said tenderly, surprising me.

I knew he wanted to hold our son as badly as I did. Had the tables been turned, I would've given him a matter of minutes before I moved in. But the tables would not be turned because, as The Mom, I was automatically given first introduction, first hold, first kiss. That alone was an immeasurable gift. That Pete had no intention of foot-tapping was more than I'd expected.

"What if he's ugly?" I asked Pete.

"Then you have an ugly baby," Pete said matter-of-factly. "He won't be—no one thinks their own baby's ugly, anyway."

I knew he was right—but would that truth hold for our adopted baby?

"We need to stop and get flowers," I said as we drove through a quaint, unfamiliar downtown.

"I know. I've been looking, but everything's closed," he said. "New Year's Day."

We pulled up to Don's address, an old Victorian-turned-office building. He answered the door and welcomed us into a reception room that felt more like a living room with overstuffed furniture, baby pictures, and Christmas cards plastering the walls. Don wasn't who I'd expected. Wearing a flannel shirt, jeans, and cowboy boots, he was tall and willowy with rounded shoulders—the posture of a man who'd been ducking through doorways all his life. His gray hair was longish around the ears and collar, and he had a Marlboro Man mustache. He led us through the front room and into his office, where he sat behind a large wooden desk and motioned for us to take a seat.

Don began to tell us about our baby, referring to him as 'Mr. Baby,' which bothered me in the way it bothers me when adults say they have to go potty or their tummy hurts. I wished he'd just say 'the baby.'

"We need to go through these," Don said, placing his hand on a tall stack of documents on his desk. "And then we'll head over to the hospital."

Taking the first document from the pile and sliding it in front of us, he said, "This will give you rights to Mr. Baby in the hospital. The same rights you would have if you were the birth parents: the right to spend time with him, to be in the nursery, and to be alone with him. We'll ask the hospital staff to sign this; their part states that they'll allow you to stay the night in the hospital."

Pete and I shot each other wide-eyed glances. *Stay the night*?

This is how I thought it'd go down: we'd go to the hospital and meet the birth parents. We'd talk in an overly polite way. We'd meet our son and get to hold him, but we'd still act and feel like visitors. We'd leave, either because visiting hours were over or because we sensed they were ready for us to go. (I wasn't sure who 'they' would be. The birth mom and birth father? The birth mom and her parents? Extended family?) We'd find the nearest hotel and spend a nervous night watching the clock and crappy TV. We'd return in the morning to hopefully pick up our son and say our goodbyes. Never, in any of my 'meeting our baby' fantasies, did I imagine we'd get to stay overnight in the hospital.

An episode of 'I'm Having Their Baby' stuck with me as a lesson in how *not* to act in the hospital. After the baby was born, birth mom, baby, adoptive mom and adoptive dad were in the hospital room. A nurse came in and started taking pictures of the adoptive mom holding the baby, with the adoptive mom's phone. The nurse made a big deal out of her being the mom, and the birth mom was okay with it for a few minutes, but then it was just too much. The adoptive mom was reading the situation, too—you could see she wanted the nurse to stop but didn't want to be rude. Finally, the birth mom half-shouted, "Well, maybe I'll just decide I *do* want to be the mom. I *am* the mom!"

So, I had guidelines in mind. We would be open and warm, but not overbearing. I would not take a zillion pictures of Pete and me holding the baby. I would not call myself the baby's mom in D's presence until she called me the mom. I wanted her to feel she had given, not that we'd taken.

Don told us more about D. She was twenty-six. She and her boyfriend, the birth father, were struggling and lived with her mom.

"There is one other thing," Don said. "Yesterday, a nurse was checking on her, and D said something like, 'I don't know how I'm going to care for this baby.' The nurse took it as a red flag, and now CPS is involved."

D had obviously decided she couldn't care for the baby; she was placing him for adoption. But when I put myself in D's shoes, it made sense that she might feel the need to explain herself to a nurse. Adoption books were full of stories of nurses trying to convince birth moms to change their minds, to keep their babies (I desperately feared our birth mom getting one of those nurses!) Maternity wards are shrines to motherhood and the mother and child bond. I could easily imagine feeling the need to explain if you were opting out.

The final item on Don's list was payment. Our birth mom's legal fees were an expense we'd planned for, and Alan had prepped us, giving us a range for Don's fees during our call that morning. Don came around to the front of his desk and pulled up a chair. Resting his booted ankle on his knee, with his caramel-flavored drawl, he said, "Now for my part in the adoption, the fees paid to my office are $11,000...if that's alright with you."

I cringed inwardly. Don's fee was a couple thousand higher than the range we'd been given, but mostly, I knew Don's roundabout, good ol' boy delivery wouldn't sit well with Pete.

"What if it's not alright with us?" Pete countered. "Are you saying there are other options?" Squeezing Pete's hand in a shut-the-fuck-up-you're-going-to-make-us-lose-our-baby-kind-of-way, I jumped in with a smile and vigorous head nodding, "No, no, that's fine--$11,000, that's your fee, right?"

"That's correct," Don drawled, folding his hands in the triangle of his crotch. "That is our fee."

I scribbled the check, ripped it out, and handed it to Don. "Okay," he said. "Let's get you to the hospital."

We still needed flowers. Don gave us directions to a Safeway, saying he'd meet us there and to look for his green Ford Explorer. Walking into Safeway, I veered right to floral and Pete went to get food. I couldn't eat but asked him to grab me a bottle of ibuprofen and a protein bar. I agonized over the flowers. Red roses, too romantic. Pink said little girl. I considered a bamboo plant, but what did that say to our birth mom—*good luck?* I settled on a full and fresh-looking, blue hydrangea. *Baby Boy. New Beginnings. Thank You.*

Back in the car, Pete tore into his roast chicken, and I washed down three ibuprofen with a Coke Zero. I pulled the sparkly pink D from the diaper bag and began threading it into the bow. We pulled behind Don's green Explorer and drove toward the hospital.

45

As we walked toward the hospital, the evening sky held on to the last of its purple.

How are we not running? I thought. *How am I not running, knowing my baby is in that building?* We stopped at the front desk and made airy chitchat with the two elderly women who handed us our visitor's name tags. My hands shook so hard that my name tag looked like it'd been written by a kindergartener.

The hospital was small. The maternity ward was just fifty feet beyond the welcome desk.

Don sauntered up to the nurses' station. I couldn't make out what he said, but a nurse came around and showed us to D's door directly behind us. Everything was happening so fast—there wasn't time to overthink. I reminded myself that she didn't need me to be cool or her buddy, she needed me to be a grown-up, a mother figure, a woman in control. *I can do that*, I thought confidently. *I actually am those things,* I thought less confidently.

"Let's go in," Don said, extending a long arm and an encouraging smile.

The room was dark, other than a soft light to the left of her bed. It was just the two of them in the room, and she was feeding him a bottle. I was relieved and worried: relieved that she wasn't breastfeeding him, worried that she was alone with him and bonding. After a nervous flurry of *hi* and *hello* and *the flowers are beautiful*, Pete and I properly introduced ourselves to D. I asked if I could give her a hug, to which she agreed, and because she was lying in bed holding the baby, I awkwardly hugged them both.

"I haven't been able to come up with a name for him," she said apologetically.

Again, I was relieved. The books said naming the baby was part of the process for some birth moms and didn't necessarily communicate they were keeping their baby. Even so, I didn't want our birth mom to name our baby; I wanted to write his name on a fresh piece of paper.

Pete puffed up and said in a compassionate yet proprietary tone I was in awe of, "We have. We're going to name him Henry Harrison. Harrison's after my grandfather, Henry's great- grandfather."

"Henry's perfect," D said.

"Do you want to hold him?" she asked, looking at me.

Thankyouthankyouthankyou. Thank you for not making me ask.

I leaned down and into her, and she placed him in my arms. He felt weightless, wrapped in flannel. Taking the chair at the foot of the bed, I laid him on my lap. I pulled off his cap to touch his hair, unswaddled him to see his shape. Bringing his face to mine, I breathed him in open-mouthed, wanting to taste his scent. Slipping his onesie over his head, leaving him in just his diaper, I held him before me, but he felt too far away. Running my cheek up one side of his belly and down the other, brushing my lips over his lips, my nose across his nose, I greeted him, "Hi, honey. Hi, Henry."

Breathing him in, I knew the pregnancy we'd lost had never been a baby. It had been a mass of cells that had never quite jelled. There'd been no heart. There'd been no soul. I could see Henry's heart beating in his tiny chest. He had a soul, and it was mingling with mine—I could smell our backyard jasmine and the scent of his tinny little-boy sweat wafting over us from the one-thousand summer evenings that lay ahead of us.

Henry had been the destination all along.

I paid no attention to what Pete was saying to D. Throughout our search, I'd been directing him on what we should and shouldn't say to our birth mom, and that, perhaps, he should really just let me do the talking, for the most part, anyway. But for the first five minutes we were with our birth mom, face-to-face with this mythical character who'd suddenly become real—the most influential words we'd ever say to her were happening *now*— and I was gone.

When I awoke to the room, Don had positioned himself in a back corner as an observer. Pete was talking amiably to D and had taken the chair to my right. As I placed Henry in Pete's arms, he greeted him in a voice I'd only heard him use twice before—a voice so tender, so gentle and fond that it actually evoked a prick of jealousy in me, followed by a surge of intense sexual arousal and the realization that, yes, of course, I want my husband to love our children that much.

Our conversation with D was relaxed. Not like with friends, but for the situation, it was surprisingly easy. She showed us pictures on her phone (She had a bejeweled leopard-print case, and I congratulated myself on selecting bling for her.). I showed her pictures of Jack and Kate, and a video I'd made of our 2013 highlights as a New Year's Eve surprise for Pete and the kids.

We asked what her hopes and dreams were for him.

"I don't know…I'd like him to have great holidays. Like if he wants a bike for Christmas, I want him to get the bike, you know? To feel that happy."

What she wanted for him was so small, a bike, and at the same time, so big, *Happiness*.

"We can do that," Pete said. "We can do that."

We asked about her life at home. She and Corey lived in her mom's basement. She helped care for her grandma, who also lived there, as a way to pay her mom back. Her parents were divorced, but she was close to her dad. He'd brought her sushi the night before; sushi was her favorite.

She took a phone call. "Hi, Babe."

"Yeah, they're here, and they want to meet you." Pete and I glanced at each other.

"Where are you?"

"So, like, another hour?"

"Okay...see you then."

"That was Corey," she said. "He's trying to start a firewood company, and he's making a delivery. He's way out, like an hour from here, but he's gonna try and come by tonight. He wants to meet you guys."

When Corey walked in the door a couple of hours later, Pete, D, and I were comfortably, lazily chatting, and Henry was lying asleep on my shoulder, where he'd been for most of the evening. Corey's eyes swept the room, and then, red-faced, jaw-twitching, he bore them into D.

Despite having a fresh C-section incision, D swung her legs out of bed and attempted to stand.

"Hold on!" D cried, her arms extended in front of her. "*Hold on!*"

Pete leaped out of his chair and across the room and put his hand out. Corey jutted his hand in Pete's direction but kept his eyes locked on D.

It was clear they needed to talk, and it was Monumentally Clear that we needed to give them the privacy and space to do that. I laid Henry down in his bassinet, feeling like I had to, like he wasn't yet mine to take. In the tension-filled scramble, we left behind jackets. Pete left his phone.

We stood outside D's door, dazed. *Now what?* Don had gone home hours ago.

Thankfully, a nurse grabbed us, saying our room was ready. She led us down a hallway, away from D and Henry. Pete and I held hands, mine cold and clammy. Corey didn't look like a guy who wanted to "meet us." He looked like a guy who wanted to take D's head off. The outcome we feared most—the one we'd never dared talk about, was happening. They wanted to keep him, or at least Corey did. Of course they weren't going to give him up!

I felt so stupid. Like I had after the miscarriage, remembering how I'd been so smug the day of the ultrasound, with my tight tank stretched over my breasts, pressing myself into Pete. I'd done it again. I'd sat with Henry sleeping on my shoulder for hours, just real casual, like that was right where he belonged. *Did I really think it was going to be that easy?* Or in baggage claim, when I'd asked that guy to take our picture with our empty car seat so I could show Henry someday: "This is me and Daddy right before we got you!" The man said, "Missing something aren'tcha?" and I yelled back, "We're going to get him right now!" I'd been audacious in my happiness.

Our nurse, Brittany, made us comfortable, showing Pete how to unfold the chair into a bed and bringing me a tumbler filled with cranberry juice, orange juice, and crushed ice, like they brought to all of the new moms. Her small gesture overflowed with kindness, letting us know that the nursing staff felt we belonged there.

I was getting ready to call Alan when the door swung open, and a nurse backed into our room, pulling Henry's bassinet.

"He's stayin' with you guys tonight," she announced.

Disbelieving, I scooped him up and turned back to the nurse to hear her news. Gina was in her fifties, heavy set, with dark brown wavy hair and a friendly face. She moved with the air of a veteran, and I liked her immediately.

She told us that after we'd left, she'd gone into D's room to defuse the situation. "The fight had nothing to do with you or placing the baby for adoption," she offered reassuringly. "He didn't know she was pregnant."

"*What?*" Pete and I said.

"Evidently, Corey told D that if she got pregnant, he'd leave her," Gina said. "So, when she started getting big, she told Corey and her mom she had thyroid problems and that's why she was gaining weight."

My head was spinning. I was afraid Pete would want to walk away. I wouldn't look at him.

The realizations hit me in waves:

Just because *this* fight between Corey and D hadn't been about wanting to keep Henry didn't mean he didn't want to keep him. This had been Corey's first contact with D since finding out she'd had his baby. The one that he didn't know about until he saw him sleeping on my shoulder. Tonight was his WTF moment. He could come back tomorrow wanting to make amends with D. He'd probably march in here in the morning and tell her: "*These two old fuckers can kindly give us our son and get on the next flight back to wherever-the-fuck Orange County.*"

The story D had told us about her contractions getting closer and closer and Corey driving her to the hospital last night, that *definitely* wasn't true. Who'd driven her? Had she taken *a cab*?

D's dad bringing her sushi? It hadn't happened. Gina said D hadn't had any visitors.

And the phone call: *Yeah, they're here and they want to meet you.* D had faked it. Her phone hadn't rung, but I figured it was on vibrate. She'd made up a one-sided conversation, speaking lines into her phone. She'd done it so well.

When Gina left the room, I held Henry and my breath, waiting for Pete to speak. I couldn't argue, rationally, if he wanted to step away from this baby. *There will be others,* I could hear my level-headed husband saying. I wouldn't be able to forgive him. It crossed my mind I could divorce him and adopt Henry on my own. But when the door closed behind Gina, Pete said nothing and, with that, said everything.

Pete took Henry, and I called Alan to fill him in on everything that had happened: Corey hadn't known D was pregnant; we were scared he wouldn't sign or that he'd change her mind.

"You just have to ride it out for the night," Alan said. "If worse comes to worst tomorrow, and D and Corey change their minds, you and Pete need to accept their decision gracefully."

Alan said sometimes birth moms changed their minds in the hospital, but once they got home to the reality of no support, especially from the boyfriend who'd convinced them to keep the baby, they returned to the original adoption plan.

"If they decide to keep the baby," he said, "you need to walk up to D, grab her hands, look her in the eye, and say, 'If, over the next several days, you have second thoughts about keeping him, we are here for *you*, we are here for *him*, and we will be here on a second's notice."

If I had to, I knew I could say the words Alan was asking me to say. I'd already convinced myself that if they took him home, D calling us to come and pick Henry up was the only possible outcome.

We wanted to be at the nurses' station at 8:00 a.m. sharp because we were told that's when the hospital's social worker would be in. We wanted to introduce ourselves, and we wanted her to like us—we *really* wanted her to like us. We decided I would go, and Pete would stay with Henry. I quickly showered and got ready, pulling my hair into a ponytail, throwing on jeans, a white tank, and drapey beige cardigan, zipping up sensible black boots.

"How do I look?" I asked Pete.

"I don't want you to take this the wrong way because I mean it in the good way," he said. "But you look like a mom."

"Perfect," I said.

Only one woman stood at the nurse's station. She was mid-to-late fifties, with a petite frame and a precisely cut, silvery-blonde bob. Her lips made a thin line as she looked over paperwork.

"Excuse me," I said. "Do you know if D is awake?"

"Who are you?" she asked, assessing me over her glasses.

Both thrilled with and uncertain of my new title, I answered, "I'm the adoptive mom of her baby, Henry."

The thin line broadened into a smile.

"I'm Dr. Hill," she said. "I delivered Henry."

My smile warmed to meet hers as I shook her hand, delighted to meet her and to hear the details of his birth.

"I'm anxious to check on D—can I go in?" I asked.

"She's on some pretty good sedatives; she won't be all there," she said. "But you're welcome to go in and see her."

I stood at D's door, cracking it open just enough to see a sliver of her sleeping in the bed. The room was dark and quiet. Her mouth hung open while she slept, making her look so vulnerable I felt I should look away. I remembered what Gina had said about D not having any visitors and thought about my hospital rooms when I'd given birth. There'd been light—sunlight through windows and a lightness of mood. Pete was there, of course, and our moms. When I had Jack, Mari was there to meet him so fast the smell of my shitting on the birthing table still lingered in the air.

When Kate was born, girlfriends from work brought a giant cookie that read, "Good Job, Mama & Welcome Kate!" For both of their births, I'd packed my favorite pillow, newly-purchased 'for hospital' pajamas, laptop, magazines, lip balm, and breath mints. D had nothing: no attentive partner, no parental support, no visitors, no comforts from home. No light. The hydrangea was there—flowers from strangers.

It felt wrong to wake her, but I wanted her to know I was there and that we cared about her. I didn't want her to feel like we'd gotten our baby, so we were done with her. And I needed her to reassure me. I wanted her to tell me we still belonged there, that our plan was still intact.

I sat on the swivel stool next to her bed. "Hey," I whispered, putting my hand over hers. She opened heavy eyelids.

"I'm sorry," she said.

Shit. *Shit. Shit. Shit. Shit. Shit.*

I'm sorry; I've changed my mind—is that what you're going to say? Please, I pleaded with her in my mind, *please don't tell me you're sorry.* I forged ahead to avoid hearing what she was sorry for, determined to say what I'd rehearsed in my head.

"That's exactly why I came over here," I said. "You have nothing to be sorry for. Henry had a great night with us, and I want you to know we're still one hundred percent committed to this adoption and you."

"I got stuck between a rock and a hard place," she said.

"What do you mean…because Corey didn't know you were pregnant?" I asked. She nodded, tears running down her face.

"He told me if I got pregnant, he'd leave me, but I was already pregnant when he told me that. Everyone is so mad at me. They're gonna disown me."

"Is your mom mad, too?" I asked.

"I don't know if my mom even knows yet. She asked me if I was pregnant, and I told her no. I kept it from everyone," D said.

I wanted to press her, to make her promise that I would take Henry home. I wanted her to say that he was mine no matter what. But sitting there holding her hand, I saw what she was going home to. A bedroom in the basement. An emotionally abusive boyfriend who'd told her he was leaving because she'd gotten pregnant. A mom who would be both furious with and disappointed in her.

The books tell you that most birth moms are in a state of crisis, and D was. I felt tenderness toward her. I feared her, absolutely—she could take away what I desperately wanted in a single breath. But sitting there, I felt maternal toward her and was happy to be feeling that way—not *acting* that way, as I'd planned to do if necessary.

"Is Corey the kind of guy who might go to counseling?" I asked. She shook her head no, rolling her eyes.

"Yeah, guys can kind of be dicks about counseling," I said, the two of us agreeing with tired laughter.

"Is your mom the kind of mom who'll really disown you, or is she the kind of mom who'll be really mad, but she'll let you back in?" I asked.

"She'll let me back in," D said.

I squeezed her hand, happy to learn she had a good mom.

"Dr. Hill said you're discharged, that you can leave whenever you're ready. Have you talked to Corey?" I asked. "Can we give you a ride home?"

"I haven't talked to him yet," she said.

"Pete's going out for some food. You want something? A better breakfast?" I asked, glancing at her tray that held applesauce and dry wheat toast. "Candy?"

"Chocolate's my go-to," she said with a weak smile.

D'd been cleared for discharge, and according to hospital policy that meant Henry had to be discharged too. Before he could be released to us, we needed to clear two hurdles: the adoption services provider needed to meet with D to walk her through the relinquishment papers, and we needed to meet with, and be approved by, child protective services.

CPS knocked on the door and entered our room as a team of two: a balding middle-aged man introduced himself as Joe, and a brunette twenty-something introduced herself as Heather. Joe was seasoned, unassuming, and friendly in demeanor. Heather was broad-shouldered, her dark, thick hair pulled back severely in a clip. She did not allow a polite smile. After introductions and handshakes all around, Joe got down to it:

"We're on your side," he said. "But the baby is being discharged at five o'clock. If you can provide the documents we need, he'll be discharged to you. If you can't provide what we need, he'll be placed into protective custody."

I felt my intestines surge and knew I'd need to use the bathroom. I wanted to laugh at the absurdity of it, to dismiss the validity of Joe's statement.

"His name is Henry," I replied to Joe.

"We'll get it done," Pete said. "What do you need?"

"We need a copy of your home study," Joe said.

Easy.

I called Emily and within minutes, she'd emailed a letter to Joe and Heather stating we'd successfully completed our home study. They read Emily's letter on their phones.

"This isn't good enough," Heather said.

My god...was that a smile?

"We need to read your entire home study," she said. "The whole report."

Joe and Heather gathered and excused themselves, saying they needed to get to an appointment across town.

"Emily can email me a copy of your full home study," Joe said, handing me his card. "We'll read it as soon as it hits my inbox."

Pete and I were incredulous that the letter from Lullaby wasn't good enough. I'd imagined that, on sight—in my beige cardigan, with Henry asleep in my arms—CPS would deem me as Henry's deeply-qualified adoptive mother. That, with all of the soul-crushing things they saw in their line of work, they'd be overjoyed to find two people so desperate to parent. But protocol was protocol. And Heather wasn't fucking around.

Pete called Emily back. I heard him explain that we needed her to send the entire report.

He was quiet for a long time as he listened to her response.

"Okay, please do your best," he said. "It's three now, and they need it by five."

"What'd she say?" I asked, blood hissing hotly in my ears.

"She hasn't typed it up yet," he said. "They did more placements last month than she thought they would, and then they were off for the holidays. She meant to get to it, but she didn't. She said she's sorry."

We weren't going to take Henry home because Emily had slack-assed her way through the holidays and not done her goddamn job? Henry was going to go into protective custody—and god knows what we'd have to do to get him out—because Emily *"meant to get to it but didn't?"*

I hate confrontation and have a deep-seated, unhealthy need for people to like me. The only time I can speak honestly and forcefully about my anger is when other people's actions negatively affect my kids.

"Do her best?" I said. *"Are you fucking kidding me?"*

I called Lullaby, hoping to get Emily, but instead, a man named Eric answered the phone, introducing himself as the director. *Even better*, my mind sneered.

"I've been briefed on the situation, Denise, and I'm very sorry," he said. "Emily and her supervisor are feverishly typing up your home study right now. They're usually about thirty pages long, and I understand we have less than two hours to get this done."

With clenched teeth and shaking voice, I stated our case one last time: "If our home study is not completed and emailed to CPS by five o'clock, *we are in danger of losing our son*."

We'd optimistically booked a 7:00 p.m. flight home that night. After the call with Eric, our goal shifted to just getting out of the hospital and into a hotel near the airport so we could be on the first flight out in the morning. Pete got on his phone and canceled our flight. I called Mari.

Shortly after, Cheryl, the adoption services provider, came in and told us that D had signed the papers without reservation. Corey hadn't signed yet, but he'd agreed to do so the next day—Cheryl had already made plans to visit D and Corey at their home and seemed confident that it would go smoothly.

After we learned D had signed the papers, our nurse, Kerry, who'd relieved Gina, came to see us. With a bright purple streak in her shoulder-length bob, a sun-kissed face, and a megawatt smile, Kerry gave off a pro beach volleyball vibe.

"I'm clearing Henry," she said with a warm smile and a click of her pen. "He is discharged. You guys can go home whenever you're ready."

All obstacles keeping us from walking out the door with Henry were gone—with the exception of CPS. I'd packed our bags and set them on the bed. Pete fidgeted while he made nervous small talk with Don, who sat with his arms folded across his chest, cowboy boot on his knee. I was sitting in a chair feeding Henry when Alyssa, Don's assistant, walked through the door with D.

"D's ready to go home," Alyssa said. "She'd like to say goodbye to you guys."

This wasn't how it was supposed to go. Leaving the hospital with our birth mom was one of those moments I'd played out in my head a million times. It was one of the key scenes in every episode of, 'I'm Having Their Baby,' and it went like this: The birth mom was wheeled out of the hospital holding the baby in her arms while the adoptive parents followed behind. There were usually balloons. Once outside of the hospital, the adoptive parents stood by with barely restrained eagerness and a brand-new car seat loaded with dangly toys. Finally, the birth mom would place the baby in the arms of the adoptive mother. But here was D, standing in our room, ready to say goodbye.

"Do you want to hold him?" I asked.

"Yes," she answered.

I placed him in her arms.

"Can I take some pictures?" I asked.

"I look awful," she said, running her fingers through her hair.

"You look beautiful," I said.

I knew Henry would want to see these pictures someday. He would study everything about her: Her long, loose, ash-blonde hair, with the few tendrils she'd tucked behind her ear falling onto the cleavage that inched out of her scoop neck. The sweet smile on her face as she looks at him, his eyes closed, two fingers poking out the top of his blanket. If he was ever hungry to find his features in her face, he would find them.

We'd agreed on an open adoption, nothing formal, only that both sides were open to contact in the future. But maybe she'd change her mind; maybe she'd disappear. We were all in the same room now, and I wanted to get the picture for Henry that I would've liked to have had as a child: *This is what your birth mom looks like.*

After I took pictures of D holding Henry, I asked Pete to take one of the three of us together: me, with D holding Henry. In the photo, I'm standing next to D as she holds Henry. I have my arm around her in a casual, collegial way—the way I used to throw my arm around girls I'd just met at keg parties for a photo I'd later put in a 'College Memories!' picture frame. If you saw the photo, you might think my smile looks relaxed, but it's the smile that shows up when I'm trying to look at ease. I think D's smile is a little forced, too. Her smile when she holds Henry alone is more natural, comfortable. But there we stand side-by-side, two women in agreement, two women who are certain, doing the best we can.

Alyssa came back to our room after walking D to her car. Corey had been the one to pick her up after all. They'd made amends—enough at least that he was still her ride home.

At four o'clock, Don's phone rang. Pete and I scrutinized his expressions without self-consciousness.

"That's great news, Joe. Great news," Don said, nodding. "Yup. Will do. And thanks again for all your help."

"Massar family," Don stood to announce, "You may leave with Henry in your care and under your supervision in all ways. You are free to go home."

I threw my free arm around Pete, squishing Henry between us. He was ours, and we were going *home*. I'd been waiting until we got the all-clear (no reason to tempt fate) to put him in his going-home outfit. I stripped him out of the hospital onesie and put him in his soft blue sleeper with the trucks.

Kerry came to escort us out of the hospital. She told Pete to pull the car around while she and I made our way to the front, where she'd check his car seat installation. As I walked to the front door with Henry in my arms, I had the same surreal and floaty sensation I'd had with my first baby. *I just get to walk out of here with this baby? And I can do whatever I want with him?*

My girlfriend, Kimberly—the most accomplished of my friends, holding both a doctorate in education and a law degree—captured the essence when she had her daughter, saying, "I love having my own baby because I can put her whole foot in my mouth if I want to."

To which I'd responded, "Exactly."

When Pete pulled up, Kerry walked outside to check his work. I stood in the carpeted lobby next to a tinseled tree, its sequenced bulbs of blue, red, and green aglow.

Striding through the swoosh of the sliding doors, Kerry gave me the thumbs up, "You're good to go, mama."

As Henry and I walked out of the hospital into the crisp January night, I took my first breath of fresh air in twenty-four hours, Henry his first ever. As we pulled away, I rolled down the back window and waved as Kerry wished us the best of everything.

46

"Can we get an upgrade?" Pete, beaming, asked the woman at the front desk. "We have our newborn with us."

"We'll need a crib sent up, please," I said. "For our baby."

After getting our bags to the room, Pete said, "I'll run across the street—what d'you want, pizza or Panda Express?"

"Both," I answered, suddenly ravenous. I'd been too nervous to eat in the hospital.

"Panda Express will be faster. I'll have to wait for a pizza," he said.

"Sold!" I said.

After Pete left, I was alone with Henry for the first time. I think he was sleeping, but I might just remember it that way so I don't feel as guilty about what I did next. The first twenty minutes I was alone with my son, I spent on Facebook. There he lay in his bucket and, if he was awake, watched me stare into my phone with furrowed brow as I chose the perfect five pictures of him and worked out the 'just right' sentiment to announce his arrival.

Pete and I shoveled spring rolls and dumplings into our mouths as we watched TV, letting our minds go numb, coming down from the adrenaline high we'd been on for the last forty-eight hours. It was a spacious room, but we ate shoulder to shoulder, with Henry, asleep in his bucket on the table in front of us, pressed against our knees.

Before bed, I bathed Henry. I ran the soapy cloth over his spindly legs and his bottom, so small I could cup it in my hand.

I rinsed the lather from his hair, washing away the smell of the hospital. And any lingering scent of D.

The next morning at our gate, I talked to a man wearing a Señor Frog's t-shirt who was flying to Orange County to meet an old flame face-to-face for the first time in twenty-eight years. They'd dated in high school and had recently found each other online and rekindled the relationship.

"We're meeting on Huntington Beach Pier," he said with a shy smile full of expectation. He was enchanted with Henry and told me he had three kids of his own.

Isn't life wonderful? I thought. *People find long-lost lovers, get second chances. People find their babies.*

The world was almost unbearably beautiful. I smiled at every person I saw.

It was one of those flights where the plane was less than a quarter full, and everyone was in a good mood because of it. The Southwest crew was made up—entirely, it seemed—of gorgeous gay men, and they went out of their way to take special care of us. Before we were even in the air, they presented Henry with a certificate for his first flight. It was the first time I saw my son's name in script.

As the plane made its descent into Orange County, I leaned over Henry, sleeping in his car seat, and looked out the window. Freeway traffic was holiday light. The sun reflected and shimmered off the rooftops and the roads in the way that can make Southern California look like a mirage. But it wasn't a mirage. My son was sleeping next to me. And we were home.

47

Henry's first year brought a tidal wave of love and family visits.

2014 was cousins flying in from Chicago, goldfish won at the Fourth of July street fair, and dinners on backyard picnic tables. It was a flight to Seattle to meet Great Aunt Pauline, floating the Coeur d' Alene River, and Grandma Carol putting her feet in the Pacific for the very first time. It was footed jammies and rocking chairs, and Mom lovingly sewing up Tigger's seams so he could comfort one last grandbaby.

2014 was planting a lemon tree in the front yard with the hope of watching the sapling and our sons and daughter grow tall together.

I watched as Jack and Kate recast their sibling roles and pecking order. Jack was tender with Henry, protective, always pulling him out of his bouncer and onto his lap. He came home from kindergarten with a tiny loom bracelet he'd made and slipped it onto Henry's wrist. Kate brought home books she'd colored and stapled in preschool and read them to Henry in the evenings, relishing her role as a teacher.

Seeing Pete with Henry, I couldn't help but remember how I'd felt sitting in Phuket Thai on the way home from the D&C: the aching disappointment—and the rage just beyond that—at the loss of our baby and Pete's change of heart on having a third child, wasted. Sitting in that booth two years earlier, this was what I'd felt slipping through my hands—my stoic, undemonstrative husband tenderly nuzzling Henry on the floor.

I knew Pete had more love to give, and there it was, pouring out of him.

Sometime in the first week or two home, I decided I would breastfeed Henry. I can say it was because I wanted him to have everything Jack and Kate had, and that's true, but it wasn't the real reason. The truest reason was that I wanted to be close to him; bottle feeding wasn't even close to close enough.

I had breastfed Jack and Kate until they were six months old. Breastfeeding is a pain; it's time-consuming, inconvenient, and sometimes painful. The first time I was ever sick enough to be scared, I had mastitis. The dates I circled on the calendar as my breastfeeding finish lines with Jack and Kate were days of utter relief.

And yet.

Breastfeeding was also one of the most sensual and gratifying things I'd ever done. Knowing my body supplied everything my baby needed felt powerful and exquisitely tender—Breastfeedingland was a milky, dreamy destination where my babies and I happily dwelled to the exclusion of all others.

Getting your body to produce milk when you haven't been pregnant isn't easy, but it's doable with a combination of prescription medication, teas, herbs, and a lot of pumping.

Domperidone was being used to help cancer patients with nausea when it was discovered that one of the side effects was lactation. It wasn't (still isn't) approved by the FDA, so I had to go to a specific women's clinic to get a prescription. The doctor there said she felt it was safe and it was approved in Canada, and that was more than good enough for me. I also took the herb fenugreek three times a day. It had a sweet, pungent smell–a blend of cumin and maple syrup– that became my body's odor; I loved it and took big whiffs of my armpits. I ate a few "boob cookies" every day—chocolate chip with a hearty dose of brewer's yeast baked in (They tasted bad enough that the kids left them alone.) And finally, I drank about a gallon of "boob tea" every day, brewed from fennel, coriander, and anise.

Along with medicine and herbs, there was an insane amount of pumping. I hired a lactation consultant named Diane to get me started. During our initial phone call, she told me she'd bring over a hospital-grade pump.

"You've never used a pump like this one," she said.

"Oh yeah, no, I pumped and froze with my first two," I assured her. "I'm *very* familiar with pumping."

Thirty minutes later, I was shirtless, sitting on the rocking chair in our bedroom while Diane attached the pump to my breasts.

I'd never used a pump like that one.

The suction on a hospital-grade pump is so strong that not only your nipple, but the three to four inches *around* your nipple get sucked into the skinny part of the funnel, and those inches of breast morph into the length and shape of a flaccid penis or a cow's udder, and it *hurts*. You look at your penis-nipple and understand instantly that the elasticity of your breast is never coming back.

For at least the first week, I sat in the TV room with my super-pump and my penis-nipples as I watched Nicole Curtis flip Detroit's Victorians on Rehab Addict and pumped absolutely nothing from my breasts. And then, one morning, there were a few drops of water. And a few days later, milk.

Since then, I've told people (myself included), "I don't think I'd do it again. It took so much time away from the kids." I almost pitched an essay titled "I Breastfed My Adopted Baby: Here's Why I Wouldn't Do It Again" to *Adoption Magazine* and *Parents*. I was going to write all about how hard it was and how if I were to adopt again, I'd spend my days snuggling my baby instead of pumping.

But I didn't write it because, while it would've made a good essay, it was bullshit. I would do it again. All of it.

I texted D photos throughout the year, but when Henry was six months, I sent her a physical photo album. I wanted her to feel joy looking at the boy she made; you couldn't help but smile back at Henry's gummy grin. But I was trying to prove something to her, too—*look here, see him, we're doing a good job*. When Henry's adoption became official, about nine months after he came home, I sent D a locket with Henry's photo and his initials engraved on the back. I knew it was old-fashioned; I didn't imagine her wearing it, but I thought she'd like having it. Knowing it was there.

FOUND

48

I'd imagined what it would be like to meet my birth mom. The town where she'd given birth to me, Longview, once a booming Pacific Northwest logging town, was a depressed, blue-collar community by the time I was old enough to be aware of town reputations. Kurt Cobain was from the next town over, Aberdeen. When our high school basketball team played Longview's and our buses rolled into town, we felt the surge of righteous adrenaline that comes with slummin' it.

I imagined my birth mom as greasy and obese. She'd answer her trailer door with a cigarette in one hand and a Hungry-Man in the other, wanting to pull me into her white trash family. I didn't want to meet brothers and sisters who wouldn't be brothers or sisters to me. I hadn't looked for my birth mom because I was scared of what I'd find, of getting *entangled*.

But after meeting Henry's birth mom, I became less fearful and more curious. When I met D, she had the power to take away everything I wanted. There was nothing my birth mom could take away from me. I had a seasoned and secure marriage. I was Mom to three kids and felt I was doing a good job. I had a career I was good at. At forty-two, I'd carved out a place in the world where I felt I belonged.

Meeting Jan at Yarn Del Sol also changed my point of view. I'd never considered that meeting my birth mom could be as simple as the single phone call Jan and her son had shared. The possibility Jan offered, that I, as the adoptee, could have control over what amount of contact felt right to me? It was a revelation. Jan herself was a revelation. She'd been dignified, someone I'd wanted to rise up to, and she was someone's birth mom. Meeting Jan opened something within me. That opening was why I sobbed when Jan hugged me tighter as I left Yarn Del Sol that day.

And there was Henry. When he was older, Pete and I would tell him that curiosity about his birth parents was natural. I didn't want him to feel like I had growing up, that mentioning, let alone contacting, his birth parents would be a betrayal. I was prepared to tell Henry that his curiosity was normal and healthy, but I wasn't brave enough to confront my own. If I was going to talk the talk, I wanted to walk the walk.

I called the Washington State Department of Social and Health Services (DSHS) in late August. I told the woman who answered that I'd been adopted in '72 and was interested in finding my birth mom. I'd called once before, I told her, fifteen years ago, and was told I'd need to use an intermediary who would contact my birth mom, and I'd need to go to court. It'd seemed complicated. And I wasn't ready. Kindly, the woman let me finish before saying:

"It's not like that anymore. In fact, just this summer, Washington passed a law that states adoptees only need to send fifteen dollars to DSHS, with a few details like your date of birth, name, and social, and we'll mail you your original birth certificate."

"My original birth certificate…with my birth mom's name on it?" I asked.

"Yep," she answered.

My heart was beating so hard, my ancient and threadbare Old Navy t-shirt fluttered as I did the math—if I got the check in the mail that day, counting mail time between California and Washington, adding on bureaucratic shuffling time, then mail time from Washington back to California, it wasn't impossible that I'd have my original birth certificate in my hands within two weeks. Fifteen dollars to find out who my birth mom was? It seemed farcical, like thinking you needed to climb Mt. Everest to find you simply had to open a door.

Two weeks later, a letter arrived with the State of Washington Department of Social and Health Services stamped in the top left corner. I walked into the house quietly. Pete was in his office, Jack and Kate were at school, and Henry was napping. I walked upstairs, sat on the edge of our bed, and opened the letter.

Dear Customer:
"Enclosed is a noncertified copy of your original birth certificate..."

I skipped the rest of the cover letter, sliding the next page to the top:

State of Washington Certificate of Live Birth
Child First Name: NOT NAMED
Child Last Name: Heth
Date of birth: July 11, 1972
Time of Birth: 8:47 pm
Mother – Maiden Name: Joyce Marie Heth
Relation To Child: Mother
Father's name: NOT GIVEN

I typed my biological mom's name into Facebook. There was one woman with her name. The woman's profile picture was of a sunset, her cover photo a quail sitting on a chimney at dusk or maybe dawn. There was no way to tell if the woman looked like me or was even in the right age range. I went to scroll through her feed, looking for pictures, but there was no feed to scroll through. She'd created an account, and that's where her Facebook activity had ended. She had one friend named Keri. I figured if my birth mom had only one friend, it was likely her daughter and my biological sister. I scrolled through Keri's wall. She was about ten years younger than me and had two young girls. She had red curly hair that fell to her shoulders and brown eyes. Having red hair (though I bleach it blonde) and brown eyes, like I do, is not common. With flattened palms, I framed up her eyes on the screen. They were kind. But I didn't see my own eyes the way I did when I looked at Jack's. I framed up her nose; it didn't feel familiar. I framed her mouth. She'd probably had braces like I had. Her lips were fuller than mine. Her smile was inviting, but it didn't feel innately familiar.

She'd posted a couple of pictures of her daughters, the oldest having red hair and brown eyes. In one post, she sat in a brand-new SUV and captioned it: "My new grocery grabber!" Keri seemed nice. I felt a pang of competitiveness.

I went back to the woman's wall. I studied the sunset and the chimney quail. I considered what kind of person would use a nature photo for their profile pic—there was no ego in that. It was also, I thought, a clue to her age. Even if she'd had me at sixteen, my birth mom would've been fifty-eight, older than the core demographic of Facebook, who changed their profile pic to reflect their current mood or political leanings. This woman was in the right age range.

I sent her a private message.

September 11, 2014

Hi Joyce,

My name is Denise, and I am writing to you about a very personal matter—I hope this letter is not upsetting or unsettling for you. I was placed for adoption 42 years ago. I was born on July 11th, 1972, at Cowlitz General Hospital in Longview, Washington. As of this past summer, Washington State allows adopted adults to request their original birth certificate, and I requested mine. I received it in the mail, and it has the name Joyce Marie Heth as my birthmother's name. I did a quick search on Facebook and found you.

I am hoping that you are my birth mom. I don't want anything from you; I have just wondered over the years what you are like and what the circumstances were in my placement for adoption. I was raised in a loving, warm family and had a wonderful childhood. My husband and I just adopted our son, Henry, this year, and we had the chance to meet his birth mom in the hospital. Meeting Henry's birth mom has made me even more curious about you and what your experience was like. I know it was not easy for her.

I live in Southern California with my husband and three kids, ages 6, 4, and 9 months. I am a full-time stay-at-home Mom, and I love it. If you are open to communicating, we can start by maybe writing a letter? Or talking on the phone? Whatever you are comfortable with is just fine with me.

Thank you so much for reading my letter—I hope to hear from you soon.

Denise

You can also email me at XXX

(I was not a full-time stay-at-home mom. I was freelancing, and Henry spent mornings with a babysitter. But I wasn't going to be out-mothered by grocery-grabber.)

I felt no need to obsessively check for her response because it was clear this woman hadn't been on Facebook for over a year. I'd taken a legitimate step toward finding my birth mom, and now I could just sit back and relax. I thought I might hear from her in the spring.

If she was going to answer, I expected my maybe birth mom to reach out via Facebook message, so when I received an email ten days later from someone named Joyce, I thought nothing of it. I figured it was from one of the new gung-ho room moms organizing a playdate. I clicked it open.

September 21, 2014

Good morning, Dear Denise.
Yes, I am your birth mother.

Ho-lee-shit.
The sunset. The quail. Mark Zuckerberg, you crazy fucking genius.

I was aware of the law change and knew in my heart that I would hear from you. I would also want to know who my birth mother is! I was sixteen when I became pregnant with you. It was an excruciating decision, but my love for you led to my decision. It was my responsibility to give you the very best I could possibly give you at that moment, and I knew a mature, loving family would ensure the nurturing upbringing that you needed.

She had been sixteen! Had I really heard that from Dad when I was little? Or had I just wished that innocent, schoolgirl version of my conception was true?

Please thank your wonderful mother and father for providing you love, joy, and care. I am very proud to see that you are passing these gifts on to your own beautiful children.

Uh-oh. She was imagining our family as being more open and evolved than we were. Mom would've swatted at Joyce's gratitude like a mosquito. Joyce had been married for twelve years but had been divorced for twenty-five by then. She loved the outdoors and lived what she described as a very private and simple life.

Your success and joy in life frees my heart of any residual dark 'unknowns' that lingered within. Now, I truly know that I made the right decision. Your life is unfolding in a loving, rewarding manner, and you are surrounded by love and family. My heart is content and happy for you! A mother could not possibly ask any more of life than to know this for her own child.

A *mother*. I bristled at and bathed in that word.

She'd lived all over the Pacific Northwest, and I wondered: *Where have you been? Do you know my college town, Ellensburg? Have you ever stopped there to pee or grab a burger on the way to the Eastside? Have you stood in Olympia, breathing in the briny air off the bay or the smell of the hops that always reminded me of tomato soup? Have you ever lived in Seattle, not a suburb like Renton, but I mean in the heart of it? What would our movements look like on a Venn diagram?*

Your precious birth grandmother was my best friend and a wonderful role model. We lost her to cancer three years ago at the age of 83. She was the light of my life, and many times, I wished you could have met her.

At last, a little medical history! It was like salve on a wound that had always pricked. It gave me a life expectancy. When doctor's forms asked for family history of cancer, heart disease, diabetes, etc., I'd always answered with Adopted, N/A.

Joyce wished I could've met her mom. I'd imagined that my adoption had been hush-hush on their side, but maybe it hadn't? Maybe they had talked about me, mother and daughter, and wondered aloud about who and where I was.

I have a poem that I wrote for you many years ago, Dear Denise. It will take me a while to find it. I have only had it out a few times in the last many years. It is time for it to see the light.

She was a writer.

I wrote back and asked for pictures. *Did I look like her? Would I recognize her features as my own? Would her hair be the same auburn color as the lopped-off ponytail Mom had saved in my baby book?*

The next morning, there were photos in my inbox.

I clicked open the first attachment, and there she was. Joyce in a leather recliner. She held a baby girl—her great-niece, she explained in the email—so tiny she was still wearing mitts on her hands. Joyce wore a cream-colored sweatshirt, and her auburn hair was loose and hung to her shoulders. The picture was taken by someone standing above them, so I couldn't see Joyce's eyes, only her eyelids and lashes as she looked at the baby, but everything about her face was familiar. She was smiling, and her grin made apples on her cheeks. I reached up and touched my own.

I clicked open the second attachment, a snapshot of home that walloped me with nostalgia. Joyce and a young boy stood on a wooden deck, looking straight into the camera. A pair of fir trees towered in the yard behind them; a chainsaw carving of a bald eagle sat on the railing. Beyond the yard was a narrow, blacktopped road and, beyond that, wilderness. I'd grown up on decks like that, eating thick slices of July watermelon, potluck casseroles, and Mom's blackberry cobbler served on pottery plates.

I took the laptop to Pete, where he was watching TV, and tucked in next to him. "Wanna see something crazy?" I asked.

He knew Joyce and I were emailing; I'd given him the highlights. I handed him the laptop with the photo fully expanded.

"Wow," he said. "That is *you*."

"I know, right?" I said, grinning.

Neither Joyce nor I picked up the phone. It was never discussed. It suited both of our personalities to get to know each other via email. I sent Joyce photos of me as a child, and she sent me pictures of my biological family. After she sent a box filled with photos of distant biological relatives, great aunts and uncles, and even a bound book of my biological family's history, I told her that while it was sweet and I appreciated it, none of it interested me. It had always just been her.

My fears about my trailer park birth mom couldn't have been further off the mark.

Joyce had a college degree, a successful career, and was still working. Construction was a hobby of hers, and with her dad's help, she'd built her home on the rainforest land between Mt. Rainier and Mt. St. Helens. My fear of being pressured to meet my biological siblings also couldn't have been farther from the truth—I was Joyce's only child.

After our initial rush of emails and pictures, I wrote to her, asking to hear more of my story.

"I have so many questions for you about your pregnancy and my birth. I'll start with just a few. Were your parents supportive? Was my birth easy/hard? Was the pregnancy easy/hard? Were you sent away somewhere? Did you hold me?"

Joyce said she'd answer my questions but wanted to write it all out and needed a little time. I was annoyed—couldn't she just whip out those few details? But she wanted to write the story out, to tell it right, and I could, begrudgingly, relate.

Joyce's response arrived a couple of weeks later, double-spaced and seven pages long. She titled it 'Your Story,' and placed two dainty flower stickers on the white, 8" x 11" envelope. After I put the kids to sleep, I climbed into my bed to read it.

Joyce was sixteen when she got pregnant. She and her boyfriend had been dating for six months. My birth father, Paul, had "blonde hair, blue eyes, was trim, and had flaring nostrils." Joyce was attracted to his smile and bravado, and they enjoyed a "multitude of unsupervised time" in the woods of Quincy, Oregon. When she realized she might be pregnant, she told Paul they couldn't have sex anymore, and their love story ended there. He responded to Joyce's pregnancy with "a rapid succession of intimate infidelity episodes with her closest friends." She felt betrayed by Paul but equally gut-punched by her "misperception of friendships."

"Paul stopped me a month or two later, after school, in the hallway. He had purchased a pair of boots for me and attempted to give them to me as an apology gift. I threw the box at him, wheeled, and ran."

I asked her what kind of boots they were. She said they were nice, black leather with stitching, but she didn't get a good look at them before taking aim.

Joyce learned she was pregnant in the fall of '71 when the label 'unwed mother' was still a scarlet letter. She'd heard the gossip about girls who'd left school for months and the abortion rumors that surrounded others. She'd seen how those girls were shunned. Joyce decided she wouldn't tell anyone—she'd hide her pregnancy for the school year, have her baby over the summer, and return for her senior year in the fall.

Instead of meeting friends after school, she took long rides on her Quarter Horse, Windy. At the drive-in she worked at, she hid behind her apron. Her pregnancy was easy to hide for the first five months, but she was voted prom princess in her seventh month. Dress shopping, her mom grew suspicious. Joyce denied being pregnant, and they found "a high-waisted formal that fit." I was dying to see a picture of Joyce in her prom dress, seven months pregnant with me. (I envisioned a pale blue chiffon with an empire waist.) Had she kept her secret, or had she been kidding herself? But Joyce said she hadn't let anyone take her picture while pregnant, not even for prom.

I'd never considered my biological mom's pregnancy with me before I became pregnant with my first child. Before I was pregnant, I thought you carried around a baby—solid, like a basketball—and gave birth to a little stranger nine months later. But at four months, I felt the first flutter of Jack, and from that time on there was an intimacy between us I hadn't expected. As a textbook sales rep, I worked solo all day, yet I never felt alone. Around eight months, I was lying on the green velvet couch in our first apartment, and Jack pressed his hand outward like he was waving to Pete across the room; I could see the outline of every finger. As his due date approached, as excited as I was to meet him face-to-face, I was also sad to have to share him with the world.

When the school year ended, Joyce was eight months pregnant.

"I became more anxious as your birth neared; I didn't want to face parting with you. I didn't want to face what disappointment my parents might feel in my actions."

The day I was born, as her mom, dad, and older brother left for work in the morning, Joyce announced she wasn't feeling well and was going to stay in bed for the day. She labored alone in the house all day and at six o'clock that evening called for her mom.

"I told her that I was having a baby. She asked if my water had broken. I told her I didn't think so. I remember father honking the horn all the way there as he sped to the nearest hospital."

I felt a surge of sympathy for Joyce's dad. Somewhere, on some level, her mom knew. But to Joyce's dad, his daughter's pregnancy may have been legitimately new information.

When they got to the hospital, the ER doctor in Oregon told Joyce's parents they didn't deliver babies. At that point, my sympathy shifted back to Joyce. I couldn't imagine being what was probably nine centimeters dilated and being told *Nope. Not here.* They loaded Joyce into an ambulance and sped her the twenty-three miles across the Oregon border to Washington's Longview General.

"Everything became a blur at that point...the next thing I remember is being in the delivery room. You were born within a couple of minutes. Your precious little cry was healthy. I heard someone say you weighed four pounds six ounces. They quickly took you from the room. They did not allow me to see you."

Four pounds, six ounces.

I'd always wondered. Birth weight is a staple of birth stories and announcements. My kids love to hear their birth sizes: Jack was small and early, Kate was big and late, and Henry was the smallest of all, and our New Year's Day surprise. It cements their place in the tribe. But birth weight isn't recorded on our birth certificates; it's part of our birth story that's passed down to us from our parents. But my parents weren't in the room when I was born, and they had never met the woman who was. So that detail, that tiny piece of beach glass I would've liked to have held in my hand, got pulled back into the Sea of Lost Information. Until I found Joyce. I knew her memory of hearing my weight announced—with the stress of the moment and the passage of forty-two years—might be foggy. But I took it. My joy wasn't in the accuracy of the number. It was in being told the story.

"Early the next morning, I got out of bed and left my room. I went to the stairwell and opened the door. I walked down one flight to the maternity ward. I wanted to see you. I wanted to make sure that I could let you go. I found you with four other bundled newborns. The nurses had lined you all up by the window. I knew which one you were. You were the only newborn without a wristband. You were the tiniest baby. You were second from the left."

She'd seen me.

Fueled by TV dramas I'd seen as a kid, I imagined that after I was born, I'd been swept away from my biological mom's sight. And that was true. But Joyce had found a way to get a look. There are no photos of me before I was six months old.

In my first pictures, I sit upright, double-chinned, grinning and clapping. No picture of me as a dark-eyed and busy-lipped newborn existed until Joyce's memory painted one for me.

I sat propped up on pillows, our lumpy down comforter gathered around me. I laid 'My Story' against my chest, reflecting on what I'd been given. To consider how it felt to have every question I'd ever had about myself answered.

49

Mom was now living in Tucson, and we'd spent the day in Tombstone with the kids. It'd been a great day of stagecoach rides, ice cream, and panning for gold, but after I put the kids to bed, I felt cold and nauseous. I'd promised myself today was the day. I'd been rehearsing it in my mind for most of the drives to and from Tombstone. She was sitting on the couch when I sat across from her in her old brown recliner.

"I need to tell you something," I said.

"O-kay," she said cautiously.

"I've been in contact with the woman who had me."

"Good," she said in a clipped voice, a steel curtain falling between us. "I always thought you would."

"You always told me not to tell you if I found her, and I thought about trying to do that, not tell you. But I want to tell the kids, so I have to tell you. (Because kids blab everything, I was thinking.) I've always been curious, but what got me to do it was knowing that someday Henry's going to be curious about D, and I want--"

She put her hand up, "No. Not necessarily, Denise."

Her use of Denise, not Niecy, told me where I stood.

"Bob has *never* been curious," she said.

"I agree, I agree...he's just not interested. And I believe him. But to be fair, if he *was* curious, I don't think he'd tell you because he wouldn't want to hurt you."

"No," she said, narrowing her eyes. "He told me: 'They didn't want me, and I don't want anything to do with them.'"

I knew he hadn't said that, didn't feel that way. Bitter wasn't in my brother's nature.

"When we've talked, he said, in a very chill way, that who his birth parents are is just irrelevant to him," I said. "If he really feels the way you're describing, that's not good. That sounds really angry..."

The accusation of abandonment against Bob's birth parents was her point of view. Bob's indifference towards his birth parents wasn't enough for her, so she was putting her words in his mouth to support her argument.

In her mind, Bob's lack of curiosity was superior to my curiosity. His lack of interest equated to a deeper loyalty. My desire to know who'd given birth to me equated to...what? A distasteful leaning toward the dramatic? A lack of pragmatism? An inferior love.

I didn't press further. We were so fucking off-topic. I'd just told her I'd found my birth mom, and we were talking about Bob.

"It doesn't surprise me, Denise; I always kinda thought you would," she said. "Especially after you adopted Henry. And I never said, 'Don't tell me.' I said, 'Don't make me a part of it.'"

"No, you said, 'Don't tell me.'"

"When you were a child, I said that, but not since you've been an adult."

She *had* said it to me as an adult, but we were splitting hairs. Do things not count when you say them to a child?

"All I said was, 'Don't make me a part of it.' And I *don't* want to know anything because it doesn't have anything to do with me. You're mine. I don't know how you did it, but back when we adopted you kids, we were told the records were sealed forever—that if you wanted to have them opened, you'd have to go through the courts to do so. This way...I don't know. People are going to be hurt. This will cause a lot of families a lot of stress."

She talked about how back in the '60s and '70s, adoption was different—that there was a stigma both for the kids that were adopted and for the unwed mothers who had them.

"A lot of people didn't even tell their kids that they were adopted," she said. "There was such a *stigma*, Denise. My mom's best friend found out she was adopted when she was sixteen, and she killed herself."

"Good lord, Mom," I snorted. "I think Grandma's friend was a little off her rocker *before* she found out she was adopted."

"That's why I was always more progressive than our peers," she said. "Your dad and I always wanted you to know that you were adopted, and we talked about it from the time you were tiny."

"Well, it's different now," I said. "They changed the laws a couple of years ago, and all you have to do is write to Washington State and request your original birth certificate."

I didn't tell her how easy it'd been to find Joyce. That once I'd gotten my birth certificate in the mail, I'd typed her name into Facebook, and there she was.

"We never knew anything about her," Mom said.

She talked about how the new law was unfair to the women who placed babies for adoption because they'd also been told that the files would be permanently sealed.

"They could always say no. There's no chance of a birth mom having the child they'd given up just show up on their doorstep," I said, even though that was pretty much exactly what I'd done to Joyce.

"And what about the birth fathers?" she said. "That's a whole 'nother kettle of fish."

"I don't know," I said. "I don't know anything about mine."

Although I had a rough sketch of Paul (and his flaring nostrils) in my mind, I didn't know his last name.

"I guess the law changed because enough people felt that it wasn't fair for adoptees not to be able to find out where they came from—that it's healthier not to keep everything a secret," I said. "I don't think I would've ever done it if I'd had to go through the court. It seemed too expensive, too complicated."

"Well, sometimes being nosy isn't a good enough reason to dig into things," she said. *Nosy* was on par with *dramatic* in her book.

"I don't know. I guess we'll see in twenty years how this whole thing pans out," she said, making jumbled motions with her hands like she was working a Rubik's cube, illustrating that, in her opinion, this whole law change thing was going to turn out to be a Major Clusterfuck.

"I don't think adoptees can get hurt, and I don't think birth parents can get hurt, but I can see how adoptive parents could be hurt," I said. Because that's what we were really talking about—I'd hurt her.

I wanted to acknowledge that I could see how scary and sad it was for her. When she'd adopted Bob, Debbie, and me, she was told she could act as if our birth parents didn't exist, that there was no way they could ever learn her and Dad's identity, and no way we would ever learn the identity of our birth parents. My parents didn't ask for closed adoptions; in '66, '68, and '72, it was the law, just the way adoptions were done. And then, forty years later, Washington State voters decided it wasn't the best idea to keep adoptions shrouded in mystery, and it was healthier to let adoptees have access to their original birth certificates. I could totally see how she felt like she got screwed.

I felt the blood pounding in my temples. My jaw was clenched, and I was already mentally searching for where Mom might keep the ibuprofen in her new apartment. I needed to start making amends, to find some common ground.

"When we took those classes for our home study, it was like eight hours of 'You have to reach out to your birth mom, you have to call her, and email her, and keep trying even if she doesn't respond. They said some people even have their birth moms over for holidays," I said, widening my eyes at her as if to say: *Can you imagine?*

"Our contact with our birth mom has been so much less than we were led to believe that it would be—I mean, that could change someday, and that'll probably hurt. She'll always be, what…she was twenty-six and I was forty-one? So she'll always be fifteen years younger than I am, younger and cooler," I said, smiling conspiratorially, trying to get us back on the same side of the fence. The adoptive mom side.

"The way they do adoption today is more like foster care," she said. "Where there's still input from the biological parents and visits. In our day, if you wanted that, you'd become foster parents. That's why we chose adoption; I wanted you to be ours."

"My adoption is no different than yours, Mom," I said. "Henry is ours. The comparison to foster parenting is a little insulting."

"Well, I'm just saying—I can't wrap my head around it, I really can't. I can try to understand it, but as I've told you from the beginning, I don't think I'd have adopted if we had to do it the way you do it today."

She had said this to me several times before, but I thought she'd been *praising* me. She'd said things like, "I couldn't have written a Dear Birth Mom letter like you did," or "I don't think we could've adopted if we'd had to do everything that you kids have to do." But this was a different angle she was coming from; she was saying she wouldn't have adopted if there was any element of openness.

"I don't think we would've done it," she said.

"Oh my god, Mom," I said, feigning laughter. "Sending letters and pictures? Not even having to come into contact with the birth mom—you wouldn't have agreed to *that*?"

"Nope," she said, shaking her head. "I don't think I would've."

"I wanted a baby so badly that that was *nothing,*" I said.

I couldn't tell if she was making the comparison between our open adoption and foster parenting to hurt me intentionally. It was obvious she wouldn't have minded zinging me right then, but it didn't feel like a zing. It felt like she might really think open adoption was like foster parenting, and that was worse than if she was lashing out.

It was after eleven. I pushed the button that started the recliner humming itself back into an upright position, signaling a possible end to our conversation.

"I only hope that your adopted child will be as wonderful as mine are," she said.

To tell her that Henry, at one and a half, was already as wonderful to me as Bob, Debbie, and I were to her would've been missing the point. She was reaching for me.

Mom knew my big secret: I was in contact with my birth mom, and I'd been the one to seek her out. Next to one of us being terminally ill, it was the worst thing I could've imagined telling her. It went better than I'd expected. I thought she'd cry.

I couldn't have taken that. That's what I'd been avoiding, causing (witnessing?) her pain. But her pain manifested as a desire to strike back? That I could take.

Mom went macro when I wanted to go micro. We talked about Washington State Adoption Laws and Current & Past Social Norms—safer territory than my feelings, her feelings, or Joyce as a woman who existed in the world.

I asked myself what a perfect conversation would've sounded like, and what I would've liked to have been asked. It went like this:

How'd you find her?
What did you have to do?
Was it scary?
Were you nervous?
What were you feeling?
What's her name?
What's she like?
Do you have any plans to meet her?
What did Pete say?
What does Pete think?

That ended up being the conversation I had with Mari over two bottles of champagne.

That was never a conversation I was going to have with Mom.

The next day, I had nine hours between Tucson and home to replay our conversation, line by line. It was hard with 'Big Hero 6' blaring out of the minivan speakers, but the phrase that kept coming back to me was *foster parent*. When Mom suggested we were more like Henry's foster parents, I'd managed to tell her it was insulting. But driving west on I-8, prickly saguaro cactuses flying by, my response crystallized. I couldn't scream it like I wanted to, but I mouthed those three syllables hard: *Fuck. You. Mom.*

But when the miles between Mom and I were greater than the miles between me and home, I knew I hadn't told her the one thing I'd wanted to tell her most:

I know that if Henry's curious about D, it'll have nothing to do with the strength of his love for me. I know that because of how I feel about you: You're my mom, my mommy, my mama. Everything. All of it. I know I'm his mama and have been since that first day in the hospital. I sat there with his birth mom, her boobs full of milk for him, and I still felt like his mom. You're a great mom, I'm a great mom, and if he's curious, it'll be okay.

You gave me that.

50

While Joyce's story filled in most blanks, one part brought up more questions. The day after I was born, a social worker told Joyce about the family who would adopt me: "a wonderful, warm, loving family who wanted to adopt a little girl."

But I was born in July, and Mom and Dad wouldn't learn about me until mid-December.

Growing up, describing the time before they brought me home, Mom said things like, "A couple took care of you for us." I imagined myself in a wooden cradle somewhere, with a satin-ribboned sign at the foot (possibly hung by helpful woodland creatures) that read "Going to Dewey & Jenny Skaggs."

I knew I'd been six months old when I came home, but the six months before I got to Mom and Dad had never interested me much. It wasn't until I had my own kids that I realized those first six months were an important time. Reading Joyce's recollection of meeting with the social worker, I had a creaky awakening to something that'd always been right before my eyes: I'd spent six months in foster care. I had foster parents who'd witnessed my first smile, my first rollover, my first tooth. I checked our computer—by the time Henry was six months old, I'd taken over one thousand pictures of him. This is the digital age of photo bursts, but still. I wondered: Who was the couple who took care of me? Where did they live, and what did their house look like? Did they have kids of their own? Would all of this information be in my adoption file?

The bottom of the letter accompanying my original birth certificate read: "If you have additional questions, please call our office at…"

My adoption file.

I did have more questions.

The state had been the keeper of not only my original birth certificate, but somewhere, there was a file that held information about my past I'd never been allowed to see. But now the powers that be had decided I could see it after all. But how?

I called the number. The woman who answered the phone introduced herself as Tami. "Hi, Tami. My name is Denise Massar, and I recently received my original birth certificate through your office. I know who my birth mom is and all that, but I was wondering what I have to do to get a copy of my sealed adoption file? And I, um, I spent some time in foster care—do you think those records would be in my file?"

I remember Tami as having a buttery, southern drawl, but I may just remember it that way because she was so dang kind to me.

"Sure," she said. "You'll need to contact DSHS (Department of Social and Health Services). We only handle birth certificates. DSHS keeps data cards on adoptees and may have info about your time in foster care."

Wondering if I was part of a greater tribe of curious grown adoptees, I asked, "Have you been getting a lot of requests for birth certificates and adoption records since the law changed?"

"Oh yeah," she answered with you-better-believe-it enthusiasm. "Since July of 2014, we've had four thousand seven hundred and fifty requests. It's important to people—the health history, especially. I adopted my son from foster care when he was two, and he ended up getting brain cancer. Having his health records would've really helped me out, but I couldn't get 'em."

I marveled at how the shared experience of adoption brought people together. I'd introduced myself as a foster kid for the first time, and Tami told me her son had brain cancer (he'd survived) within our first sixty seconds of conversation.

"I know the law changed, but I don't really know how. How does it work now?" I asked.

"Basically, the law says an adoptee has a right to their records, but the state gives birth parents a chance to say what the child can or can't have from their records," Tami said. "Birth parents can fill out a Contact Preference Form where they pick from four choices:

- Yes, the adoptee can contact me. Give the adoptee everything, or
- The adoptee may contact me, but only through a confidential intermediary, or
- The adoptee may not contact me at all, but you may give them their birth certificate, or
- The adoptee may not contact me, and do not give the adoptee their birth certificate.

But all adoptees, no matter what selection their birth parents make, will be sent their medical history."

I was riveted.

"How do the biological parents even know to fill out the form—that there's a form to be filled out?" I asked.

"The state announced the law change in a variety of ways," she said. "Press releases went out, TV news picked it up, all the major newspapers."

"*Wow.* How many birth parents have filled out the form so far?" I asked. "And what did most of them want? I'm sorry—am I asking too much? I'm just so curious."

"Oh no, honey, it's fine. Give me a minute; I got all that right here," she said, making scrolling noises. "Okay, here it is: three hundred twelve Contact Preference Forms have been sent in by birth parents. Of those, one hundred eighteen said yes, please let the adoptee contact me, give 'em everything. Eleven said the adoptee could contact them only through a confidential intermediary. Two said the adoptee couldn't contact them, but we could give 'em their birth certificate. One hundred eighty said they didn't want to be contacted at all, and we couldn't give the adoptee their birth certificate."

I felt for the adoptees who'd made the call I'd made a few weeks before, only to be told their biological parents filled out a form stating they didn't want to be contacted and had blocked them from seeing their birth certificate. Where I'd held my original birth certificate in trembling hands and felt a loop in my fabric satisfyingly close, they'd felt rejected, cut off at the knees. It didn't seem fair that after relinquishing all rights to a child, a biological parent could still reach through the decades and wag their finger—*uh-uh-uh*—and prevent their now-adult child from seeing their original birth certificate.

And yet. When those birth moms placed their babies for adoption, they were promised there was no way their children could ever find them.

I could see both sides.

"Oregon's been open for quite a while," Tami said. "And adoptees get their whole file, everything. They don't allow birth parents to say no. But what we have is good; it's a step in the right direction."

"Do you happen to know the name of the law or bill that made all of this possible in Washington?" I said.

"Yep, Senate House Bill 1525—it was written by two women, state Rep. Tina Orwall and Senator Ann Rivers. Tina was adopted, and Ann is a birth mom," Tami replied.

I thanked Tami profusely during our goodbyes and immediately called DSHS.

A woman named Debbie (that was her real name) answered the phone. She also couldn't have been nicer. (These women were in the *right role* as the frontline for nervous adoptees taking the first stab at sleuthing their past.) She said they most likely did have my records—they had adoption records dating back to 1907—but she couldn't promise anything. She said I needed to fill out an archive request form and that she'd send it to me to make it easy.

"Once you fill that out, I can go try to find your file," she said.

"Are the files on site, like…where you are?" I asked, envisioning the state offices in Olympia that sat on the Capitol building campus.

We'd gone there as kids to watch the fireworks over Capitol Lake. On warm nights, we'd pull worms from the soggy lawn for fishing, spotting them with Dad's heavy Maglite we weren't normally allowed to touch and smelled like the bench seat of his state-issued Crown Vic. Had my file been there in those cement buildings I'd been running around all my life?

"Yeah, they're here. In a warehouse," she answered. "Wait—when was your adoption?"

"1972."

"Oh, that's old," she said. "I'll have to find your data card in the card catalog first, then I should be able to find your file. We started digitizing in '83."

"Do you happen to know anything about why it might've taken six months for me to be placed? My brother was adopted in '66 and went home at two weeks, but for some reason, I wasn't adopted until I was six months old," I said. "I've been told that back then, if the biological father was unknown (or unnamed, Joyce refused to name Paul on my birth certificate), the state ran an ad in local papers saying, 'A baby was born on blah, blah, blah—any men out there want to claim it?' and after the ad ran, *then* the baby could be placed for adoption. Is that true? Have you heard of anything like that?"

"Yeah, that's called a 'Seeking John Doe,' that could be the reason, but your file might tell you more. I have a meeting now, but unless it goes long, I should have time to head over to the warehouse and find your records this afternoon."

We hung up, and I excitedly opened the archive request form Debbie had already emailed and read the first question:

Requestor's Name (LAST, FIRST, MIDDLE)?

I was stumped.

My married name, Denise Massar, would be of no help. My maiden name, Denise Skaggs, might be the right answer, but I wasn't yet Denise Skaggs when my adoption file began with Joyce's relinquishment in the hospital, so that didn't seem right. Joyce told me she'd been allowed to name me in the hospital and that she'd named me Christine Anne after her mom and sister. But Christine Anne hadn't made it onto my birth certificate. There were a couple of early Polaroids in my baby book with the name Lynn scrawled across the back, so Lynn was my name when I was in foster care. But what last name should I use? On my original birth certificate, my name read: NOT NAMED Heth.

I sent Debbie an email asking "What name should I use?"

She responded immediately: "Baby Heth."

After the initial stumper, the form was simpler than those I've filled out so that my kids could jump around in a warehouse full of trampolines. I sent it back to Debbie.

I imagined her sitting in a meeting somewhere, black hose and skirt, while some suit blathered on. I willed them to shut up so she could get to the card catalog.

A word about US birth certificates:

If you're not adopted, you have one.

If you're adopted, you have two. (Though the original may not be available to you.)

Your original birth certificate lists your biological mother's name, age, and address at the time of your birth, and the state where she was born. But, as part of the adoption process, a second certificate is issued in which all sections concerning parentage are completed with the adoptive parents' information. Your birth certificate seems like it should be an absolute document, a one-off. But it's not. Adoptees' second birth certificates are completely legal, state-issued forgeries.

Birth certificates are the ultimate form of legal identification, and the need for the second one is obvious; you can't parent without one. Mom plucked mine from the tin box in their bedroom closet regularly as a requirement for official childhood activities: registering for school, applying for a social security number, opening a bank account, and completing college applications. As an adult, I called on Mom for a copy of my birth certificate to get my first passport (and again to get a replacement for that passport I quickly lost), and finally, when Pete and I applied for our marriage license.

My second birth certificate reads:

CHILD NAME: DENISE MARIE SKAGGS
DATE OF BIRTH: July 11, 1972
HOUR: 8:47 p.m.
MOTHER – MAIDEN NAME: Virginia L. Brown
AGE (AT TIME OF THIS BIRTH): 32
MOTHER – STATE OF BIRTH: California
FATHER -- NAME: Darrell O. Skaggs
AGE (AT TIME OF THIS BIRTH): 32
FATHER – STATE OF BIRTH: Washington

Even when I was very young, I knew that the "facts" listed on my birth certificate weren't the facts of my life. It looked so official, my CERTIFICATE OF LIVE BIRTH from the STATE OF WASHINGTON DEPARTMENT OF SOCIAL HEALTH SERVICES BUREAU OF VITAL STATISTICS, but I knew it wasn't true. How could Mom and Dad's names be on my *birth* certificate?

When I compared my two certificates, the only facts that remained identical were the date and time of my birth. The name of the doctor who delivered me was the same, but there was a subtle difference: he'd signed my original because he was there to do so. On the reproduction of my birth certificate, the doctor's name was typed into the spot where his signature should've been.

We were at the hospital to name Henry, so his name is identical on both of his birth certificates, but in our tin box, we have the original with D's information and the second that arrived months after he'd been home, naming us as his parents.

I like having both of them there. One is original, but they are both real. She gave birth to Henry, and we are his parents.

As an adoptee, I'm grateful I was able to see my original. It's a peculiar feeling growing up knowing the mother listed on your birth certificate is not the woman who gave birth to you. It's a *birth certificate*, right? Your mom is your mom in every sense of the word, with the exception of having given birth to you, yet her name is given on your certificate of birth, to the exclusion of the woman who did. The truth about who gave birth to you is hidden from you—it's more hidden from you than it is from state workers in a cement building downtown. It feels like that information should be yours.

My adoption file arrived one month later. The envelope was thinner than I'd imagined—I thought they might even send me a document box like the ones attorneys use. The kids were watching Minecraft videos on YouTube. I told them I was going upstairs to poop to buy myself more time. I sat down on our bedroom floor and started reading:

FACE SHEET FOR CHILD IN FOSTER CARE
Child's Name: Lynn Heth
Religion: Protestant

I'd seen Joyce's religion listed as Protestant on other documents. It struck me as funny that the religion of my birth mom was transferred to me, as if through umbilical cord. Pete and I are pretty much on the same page with religion, but every once in a while, his Catholic upbringing enters the room, like a tiny pope's miter peeking out from behind a curtain. Later that evening, I showed him where I was listed as a two-day-old Protestant.

"Isn't that funny," I said, my voice fizzy with amusement. "That they would assign Protestant as my religion just because it was Joyce's?"

"Not really. I think it's pretty normal that babies take their mom's religion," he said.

"But she'd already given me up! Religion is cultural, not *biological*," I elaborated, waiting for his agreement to my point.

He shrugged his shoulders, which was his response when he didn't agree with me but wasn't interested enough in the topic to debate it.

The face sheet also gave the names of my foster parents, Calvin and Cherlee. (I'm not *totally* positive about Cherlee; my case worker wrote with a cursive that looked more like EKG waves than handwriting, which was maddening.) Calvin and Cherlee had two kids of their own, Calvin Jr. and Odes. Their names were so *hillbilly*. They'd taken me in and cared for me at a time when no one else would, and their names (read: their social class) embarrassed me.

CHILD IN FOSTER CARE – PERIODIC ASSESSMENT
- 7-16-72 Placed in Calvin (redacted last name) foster home 7-26 thru 7-29 Placed in hospital for diarrhea. Now fine.
- 8-2-72 Placed in (redacted last name) home. Calvin home is on vacation.
- 8-4-72 Placed in (redacted last name) home. (Redacted last name) had to leave on family emergency.
- 8-7-72 Placed back in care of Calvin family, vacation over

Not only had I been in the foster system, but I'd been in three different homes and had a stay in the hospital before I was one month old. I picture Bob and me when we were little, standing on the rocky shoreline of the Cowlitz River—he's teaching me how to skip rocks, and I am mesmerized by how they barely skim the surface.

DESCRIPTION OF CHILD'S ADJUSTMENT IN FOSTER HOME:
"Lynn has done very well in the home. She is an alert, happy baby. Eats and sleeps well—very responsive. Laughs out loud—very loveable. According to foster mother, Lynn also has a 'red head temper.'"

This detail makes me smile.

CHILD'S MEDICAL REPORT
(Completed when I was six months old, this is the first document in which Mom and Dad appear; their signatures are at the bottom.)
Name: Lynn
Pregnancy: No prenatal, full term
Apgar: One minute: 9, Five minutes: 9

There was a detail on my medical report I didn't comprehend the significance of until my second read-through, over a year after receiving my adoption file. My medical report was the first physical evidence Mom and Dad received of my existence. They would've been thrilled to learn the weight, length, and overall robust health of their new daughter they had yet to meet. On the report, my name is given as Lynn. Debbie's middle name was Lynn. It must have taken Mom's breath away to see that the daughter she was adopting shared the name of her daughter who had died. I scrutinized Mom's signature at the bottom for signs of shakiness. She did not falter.

As I read, names and dates of coincidence magnified themselves and danced on the page: On July 13, 1972, I am two days old. A TEMPORARY ORDER AUTHORIZING REMOVAL FROM HOSPITAL is filed, and I'm discharged from the hospital and put into the custody of the Department of Social Health Services as a ward of the state. Sixty miles away in a lighthouse, my dad turns thirty-three. I see him cock his head to the side and crack a self-deprecating joke before he blows out the candles on Mom's homemade chocolate cake. Dad, Mom, and Bob sit around the yellow Formica table that would eventually land in the rec room of our house on 88th Avenue. Mom is still flattened by Debbie's death just twenty months before, but she smiles brightly for her son.

On August 3, 1972, I am three weeks old. Joyce and her father appear in court to sign a REPORT OF GUARDIAN AD LITEM. Because Joyce was not yet eighteen, her father, Robert, acts as her guardian and legally places me for adoption. On the same day, sixty miles away, my brother Bob (Robert) turns six. I see his innocent, smiling face, a brightly colored cone atop his head.

Another homemade cake. Six flickering candles reflecting in the pupils of his cornflower blue eyes.

I am coming, I whisper to them.

There were statements sprinkled throughout my file that to read and understand as pertaining to me were surreal:

"Said child has no parent willing or capable of providing proper parental control and is in danger of growing up to lead an idle, dissolute, and/or immoral life."

It'd only been since my talk with Debbie at DSHS a few weeks before that I'd even thought of myself as having been a foster kid. But I had been up for grabs in the system, and several stars had to align to deliver me to my family—my family, by chance, though I couldn't imagine having any other. This dizzying consideration of chance wasn't one I attributed only to adoption. After Jack was born, Pete and I were strolling him around the neighborhood. I was drunk with new-mom love. I grabbed Pete's arm as we walked:

"Do you think about how amazing it is that we have *him*? This *exact* little person? I mean, if we would've had sex one minute later, or if you would've come three seconds earlier, this would be a *totally different person*. But that one sperm out of hundreds of millions made its way to my egg and made *Jack*."

"Yep," Pete calmly answered.

I stopped and turned him to me.

"But do you *get it*?" I asked, my eyes brimming with tears of wonder and gratitude.

ADOPTION PROGRAM CHANGE OF STATUS REPORT
(The final report stating I'd been placed in a home for adoption.)
PLACED: 12-29-72

Margaret Tack—the social worker who'd handled Bob's, Debbie's, and my adoption, becoming a close friend of my parents in the process—had signed at the bottom of the report.

And though there was no official place for her to add a comment, to the left of her signature, she'd written: *Lovely placement—*

I was overwhelmed by the history and intimacy contained in her words. She knew my parents' and Bob's heartache and what my joining the family would mean in regard to healing them. She knew Mom was exceptionally loving, nurturing, and generous, and what connecting us as mother and daughter would mean for me.

It was a lovely placement.

51

Joyce and I had kept a loose but consistent contact. Our relationship had settled into an email every couple of months, birthday cards, and Christmas gifts. Both Christmases I'd known her, Joyce had sent gifts for our family. On my gifts, she'd clipped large silk poinsettias into the bow, first white, then red. I'd placed them high in our tree.

On Memorial Day Weekend, 2017, Dad and Donna were throwing a party to celebrate their twentieth wedding anniversary, and both sides of the family were meeting up in Lincoln City, Oregon, for the long weekend. Pete and I planned to drive to Seattle afterward and spend a few days there with the kids. It was the perfect opportunity to meet Joyce. We'd both expressed a desire to meet face-to-face, and the timing felt right. She lived east of the Cascade mountains, three and a half hours from Seattle, and since I wasn't making a trip to the Northwest just to meet her, the stakes weren't nerve-crushingly high. She excitedly agreed to meet us in Seattle, and a date was set. I wrote *Joyce* on the calendar.

About a month before our meet-up date, Joyce sent an email saying that her ninety-one-year-old Dad needed heart surgery; they hadn't scheduled it yet, but it was looking like the day we were to meet might be his first day of recovery, and if so, she wouldn't be able to make it to Seattle—could she let me know in a few weeks? I was annoyed. Humbled. I'd thought meeting me would trump everything else in her world, including her dad's recovery from heart surgery. I mean, it was *recovery*, not the actual surgery. Her emails and letters had made it clear that she considered me her daughter and my reaching out to her was one of the greatest joys of her life.

I told Pete she might not be able to meet us.

I mentioned it a couple of times.

"I think you're scared she's backing out—that she doesn't want to meet you," he said.

"I am not!" I said a little too forcefully.

Maybe she was great via email, but actually a flake. Was she one of those people who made big plans and then backed out at the last minute due to social anxiety or because she had no intention of following through with the plans to begin with? I was that person sometimes, but I didn't want *Joyce* to be that person.

She sent an email a couple of weeks later saying that her dad's first day of recovery was indeed going to be the day that we'd agreed to meet, but added, "You mentioned you will be in Portland a few days before you go to Seattle and Dad's surgery will be at OHSU in Portland. What dates will you be there?"

I replied that we'd be there May 26 and 27. So would she.

Our meeting would take place in Portland where we would both just happen to be for forty-eight hours and happened to be less than an hour away from Longview, where she'd given birth to me forty-four years before. To my delight, Joyce suggested we meet at the café in Powell's Books. Powell's City of Books occupies an entire city block, has three stories, two wings, and nine rooms, color-coded by genre. I'd wanted to see and smell the stacks since I first learned of Powell's in high school. It was the number-one place I planned to visit with Pete and the kids during our stop-over in Portland, so you can imagine how serendipitous it felt when Joyce threw out, "How 'bout we meet at Powell's?"

After a flight delay in San Francisco, a rental car mishap at PDX, and getting caught in 405 traffic headed into Portland, there was no time to go to the hotel before meeting Joyce. I ended up in the parking lot across from Powell's, spraying Arrid Extra Dry into my armpits and shoving two sticks of Cinnamon Orbitz into my mouth while crouched behind our rental car, hoping that Joyce wouldn't see my crude freshening up through the floor-to-ceiling windows of the café.

Pete and I had agreed that he and the kids would grab pizza for an hour to give Joyce and me time to get our bearings with each other.

"Wish me luck, guys," I said into the back seat.

"Good luck, Mommy!" Jack and Kate said in unison.

"Good luck, Mommy!" Henry followed, catching on to his role in the exchange.

I walked tall into the café, trying to hold my face in a relaxed and pleasant expression. (What should I do with my hands? *What do I normally do with my hands?!*) I knew I'd know her when I saw her. I walked the small lap, sweeping my eyes over every woman's face, looking for one like mine. I took a table, relaxed my face, and texted her: "I'm here, in the coffee shop."

Joyce sent back: "Just looking through the stacks. BE RIGHT THERE."

I sat facing the door. I took my cardigan off, wanting her to see that I kept fit, that I had toned arms. But I was under a fan, so I scrambled to put my cardigan back on.

She walked on the balls of her feet, almost bouncing into the room. I knew her immediately.

"It's really you," I said with a nervous laugh.

"It's really *you*!" she said as we hugged.

Her embrace was easy. I was afraid she might hold me at arm's length, staring wetly into my eyes, which would have made me uncomfortable. But she hugged me like a dear friend she was meeting for coffee. We sat down. We'd already covered my birth story, and a lot of our life stories during the two years we'd been emailing, so we didn't need to interview each other; we could just talk. She spoke with energy, using her hands and arms to make a point or convey whole-hearted agreement. She dropped an f-bomb the first five minutes, and I was instantly at ease and more than a little smitten.

She told me she was taking care of her dad with the help of her brother (her mom had passed away a few years before), and at ninety-one, he'd just started declining.

"He's just grumpy and ungrateful—it's hard sometimes," she said.

But her affection for him was obvious. It occurred to me that she was talking about my biological grandfather and that maybe I should feel more compassion, more interest than I normally would when hearing about an elderly stranger's health issues, but I didn't.

"Do you want some coffee? Some water? We should get something," she said, getting up to walk over to the barista and the pastry case.

"Just some water would be great," I said. "I've had a ton of coffee today."

From where she stood, staring up at the chalkboard, she called over, "Do you have any more gum?" which pleased me in its casual intimacy.

"Yes! I do," I said. "I didn't want to have coffee breath when I met you, so I just bought some today."

"I was thinking the same," she said.

I took stock of her as she ordered. She wore white cotton slacks and a soft, melon-colored shirt with three-quarter sleeves. Sensible white sandals exposed newly-pedicured red toenails. She wore her auburn hair just past her shoulders, with her reading glasses pushed up on top of her head. She pulled her wallet from a black leather fanny pack, surely necessary to keep her busy hands free. Her movements were quick, full of energy—it was her body language, more than anything, that made her seem so *young*. I knew she'd been seventeen when she had me, so that would make her sixty-one, but the sixty-one I'd pictured in my head was much older.

"I've loved watching you and your family on Facebook," she said, placing a water in front of me. "There's no one I hold in higher regard than you and Pete when it comes to parenting or your relationship."

"We are pretty fabulous on Facebook," I said, poking fun at my sunny posts. But I wanted to be serious, to be real with her.

"Pete and I are really good partners, and I love him, but he's not my best friend. My girlfriends are my best friends. We're not *soulmates*," I said.

"We've been sold a bill of goods, sweetie!" she said, slapping the table. "It's a lie; there's no such thing!"

Whether she said it because she'd found it to be true or to make me feel better about my life didn't matter; she said it with such surety, such joy—like she was letting me in on a joke I was finally old enough to hear—that it *did* make me feel better.

Jack says my laugh is loud and embarrassing and should be avoided in front of his friends. I heard my own laugh for the first time when it came out of Joyce's mouth. When she threw her head back and laughed her big, throaty laugh, it stopped me mid-sentence it was so innately familiar.

"If you've got a true partnership, you've got everything," she said, squeezing my hand.

She told me how she and her sister became estranged—a story involving their parents' fiftieth wedding anniversary and a matter of seventy-five dollars. As she talked, I kept my antennas attuned for crazy. Was Joyce one of those people who felt that everyone had done them wrong, and then one day it hits you that they are the common denominator in all of the done wrong stories? She didn't sound crazy. I found myself firmly planted on her side.

"The pictures of Africa," Joyce said. "Where'd you go?"

"Kenya. One of my best friends from college, Judy, was from Nairobi. For graduation, I asked my family for money. Between that and two jobs, I scraped together the nine-fifty for the ticket. I ended up staying with her family for a month—it was incredible. I thought I'd be back every other year or so, but I've never been back."

My trip to Africa was a time in my life I was proud of because I was so young, because I hadn't hesitated, because I hadn't even known when I'd return (so different from me now, who books return flights with having "time to re-charge" in mind). I told Joyce I'd taken a similar trip when I was a little older, traveling Australia for a month. I was trying to impress her.

Pete and the kids walked toward the table, a kinetic jumble entering the room. Kate gave Joyce a warm hug. Jack was shy and reserved. I couldn't help but wonder if, as the oldest, he remained lukewarm to Joyce out of loyalty for my mom, and if he was, I loved him for it. Henry was running under and around the tables, too little to understand who Joyce was or why we were there.

"Anybody want anything?" Pete asked.

"I'll take a hot chocolate," I said, still freezing. Was I in shock, I wondered?

After Pete returned with a hot chocolate for me and snickerdoodles for the kids, I watched him interact with Joyce. I wanted to crawl inside his brain—what was he seeing? Did he see me in her? What did he think of her? The chatter hummed along; Joyce asked Jack about baseball and Kate about our dog. I was happy to step out of the spotlight and observe—so proud to show off my people.

"What are your plans for tonight? What do you need to do?" I asked Joyce.

"I need to get going pretty soon—we're getting up at three a.m. for Dad's surgery," she said.

"Us too," I answered. "We need to get to our hotel and check in; it's been a long day for the kids. For all of us," I smiled.

"I want to get your birthday present before we leave," she said, grabbing my hand.

It was odd, thrilling that she knew my birthday was coming up, though I hadn't told her.

We left Pete and the kids in the cafe to go shopping.

"I want to get you a couple of books by Rebecca Solnit—have you read her?" Joyce asked as we climbed the stairs, her taking them two at a time.

She saw me notice, "Do you do that too?"

I did.

"I've heard of her but haven't read her," I said, seeing Solnit's name in typeset in my mind, imprinted from reviews I'd read. Solnit's 'Men Explain Things to Me' had been prominent in the media since Trump's campaign and presidency. Joyce knew exactly where to go in the stacks.

After we left Solnit, we wandered through the retail area. Joyce asked me to choose a stuffed animal for each of the kids, and she chose a Powell's trucker cap for Pete that I knew I'd end up stealing from him.

"For your birthday," she said, placing the handled, brown-paper Powell's bag in my hands, the weight of it just right.

We returned to the café, and Joyce gave Henry his hedgehog, Jack his owl, and Kate her dog.

"This is just the beginning," Joyce said, as we said our goodbyes. "You guys can come visit me, or I'll come visit you..."

"For sure," Pete and I said, nodding in agreement.

Joyce said it was the beginning, but it felt like an ending to me. The café in Powell's City of Books was my finish line. Anything from that point forward would be something new, something fresh. I'd no longer be communicating with my Biological Mom, the Maybe-Cheerleader, She Who Must Not Be Named. From here on out, I'd be talking to Joyce, the kind, energetic, open, and irreverent woman I now knew her to be.

I felt heady with a new wholeness. I'd almost missed this.

After we said goodbye to Joyce, Pete, the kids, and I walked across Burnside, headed back to our car. My mom hadn't given birth to me, but she was my mom. She'd be okay with my wanting to know Joyce someday, I was sure of it—her unconditional love and support had been a constant fact of my life. I hadn't given birth to the three-and-a-half-year-old boy holding my hand as we crossed the street, but he was my son. D had given birth to him, and he would always know who she was and where to find her. I stood under Portland's purpling sky, taking deep breaths of cool air, feeling brave and light and free.

Acknowledgments

I sat at my desk for years, working on *Matched*, in the hopes that someone, hopefully, lots of someones, would connect with the story I was telling. That they would laugh at the funny parts, cry at the sad parts, and nod their heads in recognition of universal truths where they found them. Hopefully, you have been one of those someones.

Thank you to my first readers, the ones who read early drafts and whose encouragement and feedback helped me to shape this book: Patrice Jones, Mishelle Nickerson, Julie Strauss, Katharine Whitcomb, Deena Kastor, Alyssa Roth, and Dawn Davies.

Jane Friedman, thank you for your invaluable professional help, but even more for who you are as a person. Your mentorship has been generous and kind and has meant so much to me. And thank you for introducing me to Nell Boeschenstein! Nell, your thoughtful developmental edits and your praise were nothing short of rocket fuel. Thank you.

Thank you to the editors who published excerpts from *Matched* and other essays—Emily McCombs at *HuffPost*, Robert K. Brewer at *Writer's Digest*, Jane Friedman at *JaneFriedman.com*, Cheryl Klein at *Mutha Magazine*, and Jessica Butler at *Raise Magazine*. Your yeses inspired a first-time author, working from a card table in a poorly lit spare bedroom, to keep going.

Thank you to the podcasters who had me on to talk about Matched: Tim Elder at *Infant Adoption Guide,* Julie Strauss at

Best Book Ever, and Mark Lefebvre at *Stark Reflections on Writing and Publishing.* Mark, remember how neither of us knew the other was an adoptee when you started the interview? The best kind of kismet.

Without childcare, a creative mother cannot create. Because of our extraordinary nanny, Cynthia Nguyen, I had four hours, two mornings a week, to *think*. To write. Cynthia (Sia), thank you for loving our kids so well. Your fun, smart, sassy, competent care will forever be part of our family's story.

The best writing teachers I've had are the works of other authors. Thank you to the memoirists who inspired me with your radical honesty when writing about your lives: Kiese Laymon, Saeed Jones, Amy Bloom, Jennette McCurdy, Dawn Davies, Gina Frangello, Jayson Greene, and Lauren Hough.

I wrote *Matched* because when I was searching for a baby to adopt, the adoptive mom memoirs I read were all lullabies and rainbows, saccharine fluff. And the search I was participating in was anything but. Eventually, I found the truth-tellers, fellow adoptive parents and adoptees who wrote about adoption's beauty and its problems: A.M. Homes, Jillian Lauren, Jennifer Gilmore, and Ben Barnz; thank you for keeping it real.

Samantha Birks, thank you for giving *Matched* the perfect face. You saw the women. You understood the story. You nailed that fuckin' cover.

To my literature professors at Central Washington University, specifically Katharine Whitcomb, Chris Schedler, and Phil Garrison—your encouragement changed the course of my life.

Washington State Representative Tina Orwall and Senator Ann Rivers, thank you for taking the call from some lady in California who wanted to interview you. Thank you for being so candid with your own adoption stories. Because of your willingness to reach across the aisle and compromise when writing SHB1525, I met my birth mom. I'm forever grateful.

To the women who've been with me through it all—Mari Gamans, Marcia Schreyer, Julie Strauss, Erika Henderson, Jennifer Jordan, Kimberly Johnson, and Kimberly Huesing. You are my hype team and my sanity. Thank you for being honest about your lives so I can be honest about mine. Mar, I'm always writing to you. And Julie, "Well, why the hell not?"

D—This story, *this boy* do not exist without you. Thank you for being his first home.

Pete, thank you for being on this parenting journey with me, then and now.

Mom, I'll always be grateful you were able to read my manuscript. Over lunch, you told me I painted pictures, just like you, only I used words instead of brushes. Thank you for your unconditional love that filled me with the confidence to stand on my own, feel worthy in any room, write a book. I miss you every day. I wish you could come to the launch party. I think you might be there.

And finally, Jack, Kate, and Henry. There were days when launching *Matched* into the world seemed too hard, too big of a job. But you were watching. You asked questions. You wanted to know when my book would be a "real book." Thank you for your unreserved confidence that I would cross the finish line and for celebrating with me when I did. You are my home.

About the Author

Denise Massar is a writer, a mom via birth and adoption, and an adoptee. She regularly writes about parenting, relationships, racism, caregiving, and anything else she can't stop thinking about. Her essays have appeared in HuffPost, Writer's Digest, TODAY Parenting, Mutha Magazine, Raise Magazine, and other national publications. She's a recurring guest blogger for Jane Friedman and has been a guest on numerous literary and parenting podcasts. Born and raised in Washington State, Denise earned her Master's Degree in Creative Writing from Central Washington University. She lives in Southern California with her three kids, three cats, and one nervous Beagle.

Connect with Denise

www.denisemassar.org

Instagram @denisemassar